The Hero and the Grave

The Hero and the Grave

The Theme of Death in the Films of John Ford, Akira Kurosawa and Sergio Leone

ALIREZA VAHDANI

McFarland & Company, Inc., Publishers
Jefferson, North Carolina

ISBN (print) 978-1-4766-6410-1
ISBN (ebook) 978-1-4766-3354-1

Library of Congress cataloguing data are available

British Library cataloguing data are available

© 2018 Alireza Vahdani. All rights reserved

No part of this book may be reproduced or transmitted in any form or by any means, electronic or mechanical, including photocopying or recording, or by any information storage and retrieval system, without permission in writing from the publisher.

Front cover: Clint Eastwood in the 1966 film
The Good, the Bad and the Ugly (MGM/Photofest)

Printed in the United States of America

*McFarland & Company, Inc., Publishers
Box 611, Jefferson, North Carolina 28640
www.mcfarlandpub.com*

To the memory of my parents

Acknowledgments

I thank the following people for their input:
Bahram Vahdani, Ali Vahdani, Behnam Vahdani, Alberto Mira,
Alexander Jacoby, Dylan Lightfoot, Andrew Moriarty,
Sarah Cheeseman, Benedict Van der Linde, Nikki Greene
and Robin Alvarez. I also thank the anonymous readers
who provided feedback on an early draft. Without all
of these people, it would not have been possible
to bring this book to fruition.

Table of Contents

Acknowledgments vi
Introduction 1

Part One—Fundamental Functions of Death Within the Narrative

1. Romantic Involvement and Redemption 28
2. The Cycle of Life 37
3. The Cult of Death 48

Part Two—The Hero's Position and the Theme of Death in Battle

4. Death, Personal Conflict and Battle 62
5. Death, Group Conflict and Battle 72
6. Death, External Conflict and Battle 81

Part Three—Narrative Attitude Toward the Hero's Suicide

7. Suicide and Redemption 94
8. Suicide and Despair 109

Part Four—The Hero's Natural Death: Narrating the Past and the Way of the Future

9. Natural Death in Ford's Narrative 122
10. Natural Death in Kurosawa's Narrative 134
11. Natural Death in Leone's Narrative 142

Table of Contents

Conclusion 145
Chapter Notes 157
Bibliography 159
Filmography 163
Index 165

Introduction[1]

Death is not the end or the beginning. Rather, it is a process. In relation to fiction films, the theme of death is one of the essential plot devices that can begin the storyline, create a turning point in the plot, imbue the film with certain political assumptions or clarify its moral outlook. In doing so, the theme of death evolves into a narrative strategy that can either challenge the hero's position within the plot or reshape it.

Boaz Hagin (2010, p. 1), in *Death in Classical Hollywood Cinema*, writes, "The question of whether death [in films] is, or should be, meaningful in general is far from settled." In this book, I will study and compare the different ways in which the theme of death impacts the narratives of John Ford's and Sergio Leone's Westerns and Akira Kurosawa's *jidaigeki* films. In particular, I will pay close attention to how the hero's death, or his response to the threat of death, affects his position in the narrative. I am not interested in the stylistic similarities and differences between the films of these directors. Rather, I am concerned with the thematic similarities and differences. Christopher Frayling, Jim Kitses, Donald Richie, and Mitsuhiro Yoshimoto have written specificity about the influence of Ford's style on Kurosawa's films, as well as the impact of Ford's and Kurosawa's films on Leone's spaghetti Westerns. More recently, John Fawell, in *The Art of Sergio Leone's* Once Upon a Time in the West: *A Critical Appreciation* (2005), has explained in great depth how Ford's approach to landscape influenced Leone's filmmaking style.

The obsession with how, for example, Ford's style influenced the final look of a Kurosawa or Leone film is not limited to film scholars. Kurosawa, in both his autobiography (1983) and interviews, explained the extent to which the style of Ford's films influenced his samurai films: "I have respected John Ford from the beginning. I pay close attention to his productions, and I think I am influenced by them ... Western dramas have been filmed over and over again for a very long time ... and in the process, have evolved a kind of 'grammar' of cinema. And I have learned from this grammar" (Car-

Introduction

dullo, 2008, pp. 24–25). Furthermore, Leone pointed out that his interest in making Westerns originated with John Ford's Westerns. In his interview with Frayling in *Once Upon a Time in Italy* (2008, p. 81), Leone said, "I could almost say that it was thanks to him [John Ford] that I even considered making Westerns myself.... There is a visual influence there as well because he [Ford] was the one who tried most carefully to find a true visual image to stand for 'the West.'" Leone went on to explain the influence of Ford's style on his Italian Westerns: "I can guarantee that the characters who register strongly in front of distant horizons in my Westerns—Westerns that are in many respects more cruel and definitely less innocent and enchanted than [Ford's] owe a great deal to his lessons in cinematic form, even if the debt is involuntary" (Frayling, 2008, p. 168).

Ford engaged with several prominent social and political themes from classic Western films, such as history versus myth, nomads versus settlers, individualism versus community, the clash of moralities, the historical and political expansions of a nation, and so forth. Kurosawa and Leone likewise argued that throughout their respective careers they engaged with themes that changed the norms of samurai films and spaghetti Westerns. Regarding Kurosawa, the common belief among scholars such as Prince, Richie, and Yoshimoto is that although Kurosawa was concerned with Japanese history and culture, his films were mainly influenced by the themes that Ford promoted in his Westerns. Prince, in *The Warrior's Camera: The Cinema of Akira Kurosawa* (1991, pp. 12–13), writes that "[b]oth men [Ford and Kurosawa] were attracted to stories of masculine adventure (though, perhaps, Kurosawa more consistently than Ford); both men continued to rely on a stock company of trusted performers; and both men, of course, had a certain regard for Westerns." Moreover, Kurosawa's films effectively revolutionized Japanese period films. Joan Mellen, in *Voice from the Japanese Cinema* (1975, p. 37), writes on this point, "If [Daisuke] Ito [1898–1981] created the genre of *jidaigeki*, Kurosawa perfected the form and gave it so deep a historical resonance that each of his *jidaigeki* has contained within it the entire progress of Japan from feudal to modern times."

Studying Sergio Leone's films in tandem with works of Ford and Kurosawa shows the final stages of the evolution of theme of death in Western/samurai films. Ford and Kurosawa's attitudes toward the standard Western themes and concerns greatly influenced Leone's Italian Westerns. Also, the critical attitude of spaghetti Westerns regarding familiar themes of the classic Westerns or samurai films (such as the hero's codes of conduct, the moral decency of the family and the social ethics of the community)

Introduction

suggests that Leone's films developed a language of their own. This language offers a different outlook on the American history and myth than Ford's Western films.

Western and samurai films are action packed, further emphasizing the role of death with regard to the moralities that these genres project in relation to the history of America and Japan. In these cinematic texts, the hero's response to the presence and, indeed, the absence of death as a physical, historical or social threat strengthens or criticizes these moralities. Even though the death of a character results in his or her absence from the mise en scène, their past actions can still affect the film's conclusion.

The existing literature on the works of Ford, Kurosawa, and Leone has not studied the effect of the theme of death on the position of the hero in their films in a detailed and focused fashion. However, film scholars such as Austin Fisher, Frayling, Kitses, Prince, and Richie have created valuable literature on each director's films. They have observed and studied the works of these directors in different theories and contexts: auteurism, cultural and social studies, historical studies and so on. Closer to a thematic study of death, the above scholars have also written on violence and its social and aesthetic qualities in the films of Ford, Kurosawa, and Leone. In recent years, Mary Lea Bandy and Kevin Stoehr, in *Ride, Boldly Ride: The Evolution of the American Western* (2012), have studied the history of the Western genre, the genre's revival, its revisionism, the position of women in these films and so forth. However, Bandy and Stoehr's study of Ford's films does not pay serious attention to the theme of death either.

The present work will add a new element to the current scholarship on the works of these directors. To achieve this objective, I will design a thematic umbrella to identify the similarities and differences between the films of Ford, Kurosawa, and Leone regarding the theme of death. This umbrella consists of a close textual analysis of the films of these three auteur filmmakers based on (a) the auteur filmmaker and the artistic freedom, (b) cultural and cinematic approaches to death, (c) the hero's journey in the narrative, and (d) the hero's tragic death in film narrative.

The Auteur Filmmaker and Artistic Freedom

Auteur theory was influenced and developed in France during the 1950s by the writers of Cahiers du Cinéma such as André Bazin and François Truffaut. The initial aim of the auteur theory was to analyze and study the

Introduction

works of Hollywood directors such as John Ford, Howard Hawks, and Alfred Hitchcock, whose films were banned during the Nazi occupation of France (1940–1944). A decade later, Andrew Sarris focused his study of American filmmakers in *The American Cinema* (1968) on this theory. In the last 60 years, many scholars have engaged with the theory to study the films of non-American filmmakers as well.

Related to Western genre, Jim Kitses, in *Horizons West: Directing the Western from John Ford to Clint Eastwood* (2004, first published in 1969), argues that the Western genre has provided American and European auteur directors with the necessary artistic freedom to develop their cinematic vision. This "development of vision" contributed to the evolution of the genre. Kitses (2004, p. 1) states, "A study of the Western through the lens of its major directors, a study of its major directors within the framework of the genre: such is the dialectical premise that structures this book. John Ford ... and Sergio Leone ... these film-makers can be seen as constituting a great tradition of the Western genre." Kitses (2004, p. 3) further studies how the Western auteur directors such as Ford and Leone exercised their artistic freedom to shape the genre. That is why he later (p. 10) writes:

> Rather than an empty vehicle breathed into by the filmmaker, the genre is a vital structure through which flow a myriad of themes and concepts. As such the form can provide filmmakers with a range of possible connections and the space in which to experiment, to shape and define the kind of effects and meanings they are working towards. We must be prepared to entertain the idea that auteurs grow, and that genre can help to crystallize preoccupations and contribute actively to development. I suggest that the genre and its rules are guidebooks that shape the attitude of the auteur-director towards the genre themes.

Kitses' idea is similar to André Bazin's belief: "The evolution of Western art towards greater personalization should definitely be considered as a step forward, but only so long as this individualization remains only a final perfection and does not claim to *define* culture" (cited in Caughie, 1981, p. 26). Here, Bazin suggests that being an auteur does not mean that, for example, Ford is the only filmmaker with a personal style and vision; rather, he is a talented filmmaker who, according to the environment in which he grew up and worked (America and Hollywood's studio system), approaches the genre and at times modulates the themes of the genre in a certain way. This reading is close to Andrew Sarris' statement in *American Cinema* (1968, p. 32) that "the classical cinema was more functional than the modern cinema. It knew its audience and their expectations, but it often provided something extra. This something extra is the concern of the auteur theory."

Introduction

The question lies in which ways an individual filmmaker offers this "something extra." I believe that V.F. Perkins' arguments can answer this question; he, in *Film as Film: Understanding and Judging Movies* (1990, pp. 61–62), writes:

> The director's authorship cannot be produced by eliminating the results of collaboration. Either film direction allows modes of collaboration that can yield authorship, or the concept of authorship is inappropriate. An authorship theory must find room for a process which may enable the director to take responsibility for discoveries, incorporating them into the film's intention. It must allow for the possibility that a movie may be enriched, rather than impaired, by changes from an original concept—wherever that is located.

Thus, the cultural and social surroundings of a director not only influence his attitude toward the genre's themes and moral concerns but also school him on how to reflect on these elements. This view is contrary to the early arguments of the auteur, where there is not much space for modes of production and the director being conceptualized as omnipotent and omnipresent.

Robin Wood, in *Hitchcock Films* (1991, p. 288), writes, "Each theory of film so far has insisted on its own particular polarization.... Auteur theory, in its heyday, concentrated attention exclusively on the fingerprints, thematic or stylistic, of the individual artist; recent attempts to discuss the complete 'filmic text' have tended to throw out ideas of personal authorship altogether.... Each [theory] can offer insights into different areas of cinema and different aspects of a single film." As opposed to scholars and critics such as Sarris and Truffaut, Wood is concerned with reading the film as a text; he seeks to understand a director's vision according to the film he has made, rather than understanding the work through the director's vision. Wood reconceptualizes the auteur theory as an attitude in understanding a singular film, or some of the films of a given director, rather than the filmmaker's entire opus. In addition, certain motifs may be established between some of a director's films, but this commonality does not mean that these motifs can be seen in all of the director's works. In *Personal Views* (1976, p. 187), Wood notes on this matter, "The validity of the 'auteur theory,' as generally understood, seems to me at once confirmed and qualified—there being, one might say, as many qualifications as there are movies. What I would like to see take place in criticism is a return from 'auteurs' to films." Wood further repositions an auteur director according to his social and cultural environment. This point means, for example, that Italian culture would influence Leone's Westerns. In short, an auteur such as Leone is not

Introduction

a new culture but an agent of a specific culture. Being an auteur does not mean that one individual can change the entire conventions of a specific genre; instead, he or she can affect a filmmaking tradition and push the boundaries, so an auteur is not a revolutionary but a reformist of the genre. Wood (1991, pp. 292–293) points out, "It is only through the medium of the individual that ideological tensions come to particular focus, hence become of aesthetic as well as sociological interest. I argue that works are of special interest when (a) the defined particularities of an auteur interact with specific ideological tension and (b) the film is fed from more than one generic source." This idea opposes the earlier accounts of auteurism, in which all aspects of an auteur work are original. Kitses (2004, p. 13), well aware of this fact, writes, "Arguments have now been made that genres are differentiated branches of the same narrative system rather than the discrete traditions isolated studies suggest, and that genre may be closer to an individual process rather than a system of fixed forms." He (2004, p. 14) further writes that, "at its core, western marries historical and archetypal elements in a fruitful mix that allows different film-makers a wide latitude of creative play." So, Kitses suggests that the Western genre is a site in which different filmmakers can portray and develop their personal vision; therefore, instead of abandoning the auteur theory, Kitses reconceptualizes it.

I believe that, among the scholars who have engaged with the auteur theory, Wood privileges his readers with a clearer view of this theory. First, he does not offer a demeaning and negative interpretation of the auteur. He acknowledges the historical importance of the theory. Also, again and again, he puts forward the idea that, in film studies, films (rather than directors) should be the focus. In such a view, all kind of theories (including those that are not directly linked to films) can be useful depending on what the researcher aims to achieve. Third, Wood manages to overcome the dilemma of who is an auteur or who can be an auteur. This is a significant point for this book, since all three directors with whom I am concerned are recognized as auteurs. I do not intend to say why they are great directors; I want to move away from a pure auteurist approach to their films. My goal is to read and understand the theme of death and its subthemes in the films of these directors, as well as how these themes reflect on their social and cultural environments. This is where Wood's notion is enlightening: the auteur theory can be useful in the case of directors of commercial films who work within the studio system.

Sarris understands the complex relationship between individual filmmakers and studio system. He is aware that auteur directors are working

Introduction

within the limits of studios. Sarris (1968, p. 20) writes, "[The studio system] connotes conformity rather than diversity, repetition rather than variation." I argue that the conformity about which Sarris speaks is another clue for studying the films of Ford, Kurosawa, and Leone with respect to each director's social and cultural surroundings. The notion of death and the reactions of the living to this concept can differ from culture to culture. My question here is how three sets of cultural attitudes impact the functions of the theme of death in the films of these auteur directors. The answer lies in their artistic freedom. However, this begs another question: How does this freedom work?

Sarris, as cited in in Bill Nichols' *Movies and Methods* (1976, p. 247), provides the following response to the question of artistic freedom:

> The auteur theory values the personality of a director precisely because of the barriers to its expression. It is as if a few brave spirits had managed to overcome the gravitational pull of the mass movies. The fascination of Hollywood movies lies in their performance under pressure. Actually, no artist is ever completely free, and art does not necessarily thrive as it becomes less constrained. Freedom is desirable for its own sake, but it is hardly an aesthetic prescription.

Sarris argues that artistic freedom is an ideal, not the reality. "Freedom" in this sense means that a filmmaker is not fully free to show what he or she wants to express. There are always pressures and obstacles that affect the work of an artist. That is why modern film criticism sees an auteur not as a figure of total freedom but as an intelligent person who manages to bypass the difficulties of filmmaking and create a good product. Being an auteur director does not mean crafting a film that is aesthetically or thematically perfect; it is about making a perfect film under the circumstances in which that film is being made. Social norms have a great part to play in this scenario. Andrew Britton (2009, p. 431), in his article "The Philosophy of the Pigeonhole: Wisconsin Formalism and 'The Classical Style'" (included in *Britton on Film*), considers these norms a significant element that has a crucial impact on the films of an auteur:

> Artistic norms are cultural norms, and the deployment of them cannot be identified in any simple way with a process of individualization or "self-expression" … To work with such norms is to work on and, in the major cases, to modify and change the terms of public discourse which structures sensibility and which governs the ways in which art is able to signify, and engage with, the existing social world. No artist who impresses us as having major distinction relates to the norms of an artistic practice as structures external to him-or herself which are there to be appropriated and "applied."

Introduction

The most intriguing aspect of Britton's idea is that "artistic norms are cultural norm." An artist is an agent of a specific culture, and an auteur is an agent who modifies some aspects of the said specific culture. I further argue that cultural conventions create habitual methods of thinking in a director. This is not a negative or positive situation; rather, it is a situation that molds the director's treatment of different themes. Directors like Ford, Kurosawa, and Leone managed, while working within this system of cultural methods of thinking, to add something extra to it. This idea goes back to my earlier argument that a studio-based auteur's films contribute to the evolution of the genre conventions. Thus, a triad can be suggested: cultural norms, the studio system, and the individual filmmaker. The latter may be unconscious of the fact that he is influenced significantly by the two former elements. However, if a director has some new ideas, the triadic machine can move and evolve.

Britton's arguments bring us back to what was said earlier: Filmmakers, whether they work in America, Japan, Italy, or elsewhere, follow their country's culture. Although auteur directors are not responsible for making new cultures, they have influenced the thematic concerns of their national cultures.

I now ask another question: To what degree can a director such as Ford, Kurosawa, or Leone exercise his artistic freedom within the production norms of the American, Japanese, and Italian studio systems? The answer is that the Japanese studio system is director oriented, in contrast to the Hollywood and Italian studio systems (which are producer oriented). Joseph Anderson and Donald Richie, in *The Japanese Film* (1982, pp. 346-347), note that "the Japanese [film] industry operates under what it calls the 'director system' rather than under the 'producer system,' which is so common in the west. What the Japanese mean by 'producer system' is that the responsibility for both the type and conception of a film is delegated by the company to an individual who selects the story, director, and cast and who is in general responsible for the final shape of a given film." In addition, Anderson and Richie point out that

> the "producer system" in essence means that rather having a few geniuses making a few outstanding films, there will be a large number of merely competent directors turning out a predictable number of competent films. Obviously, as in any film industry, the really outstanding movie is the exception rather than the rule, and just as obviously-it is usually the responsibility, if not the entire conception of a single man. It is these single men, all over the world, who have created the art of the film [1982, p. 350].

Introduction

I am not in favor of using the concept of "few geniuses" in branding directors. It results in a biased view that some directors are better than others in terms of intellectual powers. Even if such branding may have some merit, it creates the same unsatisfactory explanations that the early accounts of the auteur theory have produced for film scholarship. Moreover, the unsuccessful adaptation of western film production caused the Japanese studios to base their filmmaking system on the directors; as Anderson and Richie write (1982, p. 347):

> The director system was found much more congenial to Japan. Under this system, the head of the studio, or very often the head of the company as is the case with Shochiku's Kido and Daiei's Nagata, is the active director of policy as to precisely what kind of pictures will be made. The responsibility for delegating details to a producer is not exercised. The director is responsible for everything in a film and reports directly to the head of the production. Hence it is called the director system.

Furthermore, on the same page, Anderson and Richie claim that "in Japan, film directors are not called *enshutsusha*, the Japanese word which would most closely correspond to the English meaning, but *kantokusha*, which has the wider meaning of superintendent, overseer, or person-in-charge." So, it can be said that the power over the final look of the film (which has been debated long enough with regard to classic Hollywood auteurs) was a characteristic of major Japanese filmmakers such as Kurosawa, Mizoguchi, and Ozu.

The great power of the Japanese director was not permanent. Anderson and Richie (1982, pp. 349–350) explain the matter as follows: "Yet, though the Japanese directors have more control of their product than most directors of other countries, the recent [the late 1970s, early 1980s] 'rationalization' of the industry has weakened their position. They are more and more tending to lose their power both to individual producers and to over-all production head of each company." Be that as it may, Kurosawa wrote, directed and produced most of his films during the era of the director system (the 1950s and 1960s). Therefore, he had more freedom to control his projects than most American and Italian directors.

Hero's Journey in the Narrative

The American mythologist Joseph Campbell (1904–1987) dedicated his academic career and writings to developing the concept of archetypal

Introduction

myths and heroes. His major contribution to the cultural anthropology is the monomyth theory, which is based on Charles-Arnold Kurr van Gennep's *Les rites de passage* (1909). Campbell, in *The Hero with a Thousand Faces* (2008, first published in 1949), writes about the similarity of myths and literature in different cultures around the globe. Levi-Strauss' ideas in *Myth and Meaning* (1978, p. 19) support Campbell's theory of universal archetypes: "It is probably one of the many conclusions of anthropological research that, notwithstanding the cultural differences between the several parts of mankind, the human mind is everywhere one and the same and that it has the same capacities. I think this is accepted everywhere."

Robert Ellwood, Valerie Estelle Frankel, Lesley Northup and others have criticized Campbell's writings in general, and his monomyth theory in particular, for their masculine tone, structuralist nature, dense language, and lack of attention to those historical and social elements that vary between cultures. However, none of these are a reason to invalidate monomyth theory in relation to studying classic films. The films that are the focus of my book have very straightforward structures. Their message is masculine and direct, with no or little ideological ambiguity. Campbell's theory merges well with the narrative of these films. Moreover, the prominent level of thematic similarity between the films of Ford, Kurosawa, and Leone requires the use of the relevant theory in studying them. Campbell's views on the similarity of certain concepts among most civilizations are in line with my book's concerns.

Campbell identifies the concept of rebirth as one of the most prominent themes in myths, legends, religious scriptures and other written ancient, medieval, and classic texts. I argue that films likewise engage with the theme of rebirth (or, as I shall call it in this book, the cycle of life) to show that the hero's death (or a decent individual's death) does not cause the destruction of a moral community; the cycle of life contributes to the biological and moral survival of humans.

The second similar idea among all cultures, according to Campbell's monomyth theory, is that in written and visual texts, from ancient occidental and oriental civilizations to contemporary societies, the audience witnesses the actions of an archetypal hero, who undergoes life-changing experiences in a process that mythologists call "the hero's journey." In films, this journey/voyage/odyssey portrays the evolution of such an archetypical hero. However, the issue of cultural difference can arise when, for example, the hero of action/epic films is a samurai in a Japanese period film or a cowboy in an American Western film. Although there are cultural and his-

Introduction

torical differences between these two types of heroes, there is one initial similarity between them: they are both warriors who undertake a personal journey that will affect their personalities and the future of their surroundings.

The journey motif is another common theme between samurai and Western films. However, the quality of this journey and its moral outcome can differ from culture to culture. During the various stages of this journey, the archetypical hero faces ordeals that challenge the limits of his physical, ethical and psychological strength. The hero must respond to these ordeals in order to complete his journey. Campbell (2008, p. 39) writes on the nature of the hero's journey, "[It] is a labor not of attainment but of reattainment, not discovery but rediscovery. The godly powers sought and dangerously won are revealed to have been within the heart of the hero all the time." Campbell's elaborate and somewhat flowery language should not daunt us. Such rhetoric could frighten the most experienced of film scholars or the most hardworking of film students to the point of intellectual paralysis. However, a moment of intellectual reflection will reveal the simplicity and ingenuity of Campbell's words: the concept of journey in the monomyth theory is not a creative force that gives birth to new and previously nonexistent qualities in the hero—rather, the journey is the trigger that unleashes the already-existing but hidden qualities of the hero.

Susan Mackey-Kallis, in *The Hero and the Perennial Journey Home in American Film* (2001), integrates Campbell's theory with the study of the journey motif in American films. Since her methodology is based on Campbell's writings on the universal hero, her findings are relevant to the heroes of non–American popular films as well. Mackey-Kallis (2001, p. 13) argues that in American fiction films, the mythical journey of the hero consists of his separation from his "immediate home," followed by traveling through the obstacles of what she calls a "wasteland" and defeating those obstacles in order to arrive at a new home. She further writes:

> [The hero's journey] moves the individual out from unknown territory (the parochial/the home/ego-consciousness) to unknown territory (often a descent into strange or terrible lands/unconsciousness) where the individual is sometimes aided (mentors/gods/shamans/dreams), and is often sorely tested (demons/shadow-self), in a search for a treasure or boon (gold/grail/enlightenment/individuation) that the individual then shares with the culture upon returning home (cultural enlightenment/awareness of the undivided nature of being/transconsciousness).

The immediate home that Mackey-Kallis is concerned with is not limited to the hero's birthplace, his family or even his occupation. As she

Introduction

declares, home refers to the hero's original state of mind, which will change during the journey; consequently, the hero will ultimately reach a new home/perspective. For example, in Leone's *A Fistful of Dollars* (1964), the unnamed hero is a loner and outsider coming into the wasteland that is Saint Miguel, motivated by the idea of earning a fortune. By the film's conclusion, however, he has reached a new home/mindset, as he is not solely driven by gaining a monetary prize but also motivated to defend innocent people.

The idea of "wasteland" is the second notion in Mackey-Kallis' theory that requires clarification. I suggest that a "wasteland" can be a dangerous location, a backward community, or even an unethical way of thinking. Only villains can triumph in the wasteland. It requires a savior/hero—not a celestial one, but an earthly one—to cleanse the wasteland of the forces of the antagonist. This change can lead to a flourishing community/society. One key factor is that, in Western films, viewers do not necessarily witness on screen the garden that comes out of the wasteland. The destruction of the evil (both physically and ethically), as is the case with most classic Western films, is the merely first step in building this ideological garden.

In non-American films, the hero does not always win wasteland back from the villains. Nonetheless, the hero challenges the villains and their false morality. This is particularly true in the case of some of Kurosawa's films, in which the villain survives in spite of this challenge. Kurosawa's *The Bad Sleep Well* (1960) deals with the corrupt world of businessmen in contemporary Japan. Although the villain survives the threat of death, by the film's conclusion his financial corruption is known to his only son. As a result, the son abandons the father. The villain also has lost his peace of mind; as he informs his superior, he "can no longer sleep well." Therefore, the moral wasteland still has a chance to be purified from evil if a new hero follows in the moral footsteps of the fallen hero.

Mackey-Kallis furthers her theory by suggesting different quests that a hero might undertake in changing his home/mentality. These quests, which contribute to the hero obtaining knowledge of his abilities, consist of the creation quest, the coming-of-age quest, the sacred marriage quest, and the grail quest. These are the hero's goals, and, as such, they form the energy that pushes the hero forward in the story.

In Mackey-Kallis' theory, the creation quest concerns the cycle of life: birth, death and the subsequent birth of both new mentality and new individuals, which compensate for the death of old attitudes (moralities) or deceased people. The point of this quest in classic films is that the hero

Introduction

most likely gains a positive set of morals by losing a negative trait or motif. In Ford's *Stagecoach*, by the end of the film, Ringo is no longer a fugitive from the law; instead, he is the typical Fordian hero who's ready to pay for his past mistakes before settling down and starting a family on a farm.

The coming-of-age quest focuses on the hero's separation from his old self/home/society and freedom from a womb that symbolizes old attitudes/mentalities/goals. Through engaging with ordeals during his journey, he matures and learns to trust in his own ability to survive. In Kurosawa's *Sanjuro*, for example, the anonymous hero evolves from a violent swordsman to a prudent warrior who avoids unnecessary killing.

The sacred marriage quest marks the triumph in separating oneself from the original home and society. It is also the reward of the male hero and, indeed, the female heroine. After overcoming the obstacles and ordeals of the wasteland and vanquishing the villains, marriage (beyond being the ideologically endorsed sexual bond among couples) will be the celebration that epitomizes the destruction of the villain(s). For example, in *Stagecoach*, Ringo and Dallas abscond after they have overcome various ordeals.

The grail quest marks the hero's redemption from his past criminal actions and shows his successful attempt to defeat the villains. In this quest, the hero's actions have a positive impact on his personal life and the community/group to which he is related. Ethan in *The Searchers* (1956) is an outsider and a racist; nonetheless, he is still Debbie's uncle. She is, therefore, the grail that he chases after once the evil outsiders/Indians have kidnapped her. In the journey to find her, Ethan rediscovers his sense of humanity. Toward the end of the film, rescuing Debbie (Natalie Wood) from the Indians establishes the hero's emancipation from racism.

The significant point about these quests is that they exist in tandem. They can be different methods to push forward the film's story. For instance, a love story can be a marriage quest, progressing parallel with a grail quest: Wyatt Earp is in love with Clementine in *My Darling Clementine* (1946), but he also seeks out his brother's murderers.

The next point is that, in different cinematic cultures, some of the details of the hero's evolution throughout the narrative can differ. In the case of Japanese period films, the main difference is the absence of the romantic ending found in most American films. Sybil Anne Thornton, in *The Japanese Period Film* (2008), believes that although "winning" a battle is an important trait of the Japanese hero in the period drama films, many of these heroes suffer a tragic fate. The novel thought behind this theory is that Thornton engages with the often-somber ending of Japanese hero

Introduction

as a means of categorizing the heroes in Japanese period films into three types: tragic hero, anti-hero, and social hero. I disagree with seeing heroes in such fixed categories; nonetheless, Thornton's categorization of the Japanese heroes is a useful framework. I am also aware that some heroes (for example, those in Kurosawa's films) have the potential to be more diverse and complex. A Kurosawa hero can be a fusion of a tragic hero and a social hero, and not even limited to period drama genres (e.g., Kōichi Nishi [Toshiro Mifune] in *The Bad Sleep Well*).

Thornton (2008, pp. 51–52) classifies the tragic hero as one who is "victimized by political slander, defeated and slain on the battlefield, or sentenced to death for carrying out an illegal revenge[;] the Japanese hero falls, loses all there is to lose in life, and dies in great resentment and suffering. The tragic hero is portrayed as conventionally noble and done in by villains, traitors, or fate." The tragic hero's destiny is quite similar to that of the heroes of the works of literature inspired by the historical incident of the 47 retainers. Thornton (2008, p. 31) summarizes the incident as follows: "On January 30, 1703, forty-seven former vassals of Naganori Asano (1655–1701) of Ako (in what is now Hiroshima prefecture) broke into the residence of Yoshinaka Kiro (1641–1703), master of ceremonies to the shogunal house, and took his head to avenge the sentence of ritual suicide imposed on their lord and carried out some twenty months before. Forty-six committed suicide on March 20, 1703 [only one of them did not kill himself]." These historical figures remained true to their former masters to the extent that it led to their physical destruction. Nevertheless, from the perspective of Japanese morality and samurai codes of honor, they were the victors. Therefore, their tragic deaths do not mean that their actions were futile. The social impact of their efforts, thanks to works of art, has survived.

The second type of hero in Thornton's work (2008, p. 53) is the anti-hero/nihilistic hero: "These protagonists are dropouts, outcasts, and criminals. They tend to be youngish, scruffy ... and so totally contemptuous of society as to commit the most heinous of crimes, despite the fact that they are, more often than not, members of the *bushi* caste [samurai]. Whether through mental illness ... desperation ... betrayal ... or disenfranchisement ... they have become totally alienated from society and its values." Ian Buruma (1984, p. 208) likewise argues that popular heroes in Japanese culture are those who, similar to the anti-hero, are not part of mainstream society: "[In Japanese culture] a large number of popular heroes are drifters, outsiders with no fixed abode, forever going on to the next place.... The

Introduction

ronin, who make up the majority of samurai heroes, were 'wave men,' wandering around more or less at random." I suggest that Buruma and Thornton, in general, refer to the same type of hero. However, Buruma's ideas are less problematic, since he suggests the overall characteristics of the anti-hero rather than how he looks (as indicated by Thornton). I criticize Thornton's approach, for, if the films avoid providing the audience with the background story of the anti-hero (which would suggest any betrayal or desperation for the hero), this does not portray him as a nihilistic hero. Kurosawa in *Yojimbo* does not inform the viewers of the hero's real name, let alone the history of his life. However, the hero in this film is still "youngish," "scruffy" and in conflict with class and social values.

The third type of Japanese period film hero is the social hero. Thornton (2008, p. 53) notes that "[the social hero] is usually based on a historical figure: lords and magistrates of the upper-samurai rank ... prominent merchants ... and even gang bosses[.] In the films, as established figures, they tend to be middle-aged or aged (a blessing for stars growing out of their lean and mean looks), impeccably dressed and groomed, benevolent, kind to children, and surrounded by younger, adoring disciples who help them solve people's personal problems as well as murder mysteries." Once more, some of Thornton's descriptions can be useful for identifying the hero, but there are lingering questions. The hero in *Ikiru* (1952) is kind, old and helpful. He is not a hero of a period drama film, but he is still a social hero, as he shows concern for the well-being of other human beings. By contrast, Hidetora Ichimonji (Tatsuya Nakadai), the main hero of *Ran* (1985), inspired by both Shakespeare's *King Lear* and Japan's medieval history, is a tragic hero. He is old and blessed with political power and devoted disciples (the initial characteristics of the social hero). However, the tragic aspect of *Ran* lies in the fact that the hero's pride and selfishness cause political turmoil in his realm. In doing so, he misses the opportunity to be the type of protagonist that, in Thornton's theory, would primarily have the characteristics of a social hero.

Cultural and Cinematic Approaches to Death

Philippe Aries, the French historian and anthropologist, reinvigorated the scholarship of the attitude of westerners toward death. His major books include *Western Attitudes toward Death: From the Middle Ages to the Present* (1976) and *The Hour of Our Death* (1981).

Introduction

Among Aries' ideas about death, there is one point that is particularly relevant to my work. He identifies four historical stages in European and North American attitudes toward death: tamed death (from antiquity until the Middle Ages); one's own death (from the Middle Ages until the mid-18th century); thy or other person's death (from the 18th century until the early 20th century); and forbidden/private death (current era). Western films are concerned with stories that occur mainly in 19th-century America (the period of "thy death"); however, the actual productions occurred during the fourth stage (the era of forbidden death). Both Ford and Leone, as Kitses (2004), Frayling (2000) and others suggest, used the genre as a strategy for telling stories that supposedly happened in the past, but the values and moralities of the characters are relatable to the present time. Since most of Ford's and some of Leone's heroes have no fear of the threat of death (similar to the heroes of ancient and medieval literature), their deaths are like Aries' idea of "tamed death." This scenario is also due to the norms of Western genre, which, like other action-based genres, depict or treat the threat of death as a normal aspect of its characters' lifestyles—whether a sheriff, a cavalry officer, or a bounty hunter, they all face the threat of death.

Related to films, Hagin (2010, pp. 4–5) offers three structures that death creates for the storyline: "It can be an *initial death*, which begins a storyline and is a cause of subsequent events; an *intermediary death*, which is both an effect and a cause within a storyline; and a *story-terminating death*, which ends a storyline and is an effect of previous events."[2] He additionally views the process of dying as a strategy for showing enlightenment within the structure of Hollywood films: "For Plato, it was the philosopher, the knower, who had to die in order to gain knowledge of the pre-existing truth" (p. 12). In Ford's Westerns, this knowledge is often the moral and political righteousness of the American nation.

Hagin (2010, pp. 12–13) applies his theory to the opus of classical Hollywood:

> In classical Hollywood films, death can bring about a shift from ignorance to knowledge. It can be a discovery of new information or the disclosure of a secret. It can also be more of a change in attitude than in the actual information that is known, the complex epistemology of growing up or coming out, a shift from falsehoods to honesty, from self-delusion and childish lack of responsibility to acknowledgment and accountability, and from disavowal, avoidance, belittling, make-belief, playing, joking, pretence, or "passing" to call for authenticity and genuineness.

The above quote leads us to one of the major themes in Hagin's theory—that death, as a part of everyday reality, shapes the morality of society:

Introduction

"Mortality seems to purify falsehoods of the past. It is as if the arrival of the death itself, the real event, somehow puts an end to games, illusions, and lies. The importance, the grave seriousness, of death could allow no more of those deceptions" (2010, p. 18). This function of the theme of death is visible in Ford's films, where the threat of death challenges the way a society or community perceives itself. The death of either the villain (who tries to harm the community) or the hero (who protects the community from harm) functions as a wake-up call for the community to become aware of the dangers that threaten its safety.

Hagin furthers his study of the theme of death in classic films in contextualizing the "cult of death" as a subtheme of death. He formulates this notion based on the ideas of the French philosopher and sociologist Jean-François Lyotard regarding the concept of "beautiful death" in the Athenian civilization. The cult of death in genre films means that once a moral character is dead, his family members or friends form a cult to propagate his memory. In action genres, the cult of death usually accompanies a revenge motif. In the end, by obliterating society's villains, the hero (whether consciously or unconsciously) betters the community and society. The idea of the cult of death is not limited to western culture and art; as this study will demonstrate, this philosophy is shared by most cultures.

Regarding Japanese attitude toward a warrior death, three of the historically significant Japanese books that have contextualized the relation between a Japanese warrior and death are Miyamoto Musashi's *The Five Rings* (2012), Inazo Nitobe's *Bushido: The Soul of Japan*[3] (2001), and Yamamoto Tsunetomo's *Hagakure* (2008). The samurai codes of honor and conduct that have significantly influenced Japanese period films, including Kurosawa's films, oblige the members of the warrior class to be at peace once they encounter death. As we shall see, Kurosawa has a critical approach toward the samurai codes. For this reason, he characterizes his heroes and villains as individuals who typically do not follow these codes to the letter.

Speaking of the cultural ethos of the religious attitude toward a warrior's death in the Japanese culture, Nitobe (2001, p. 11) writes, "[Buddhism] furnished a sense of calm trust in fate, a quiet submission to the inevitable, that stoic composure in sight of danger or calamity, that disdain of life and friendliness with death." This idea is similar to the idea of tamed death in western thought because, as Aries (1976, p. 13) suggests, death is always "close" and "near" in the minds of people. Also, Campbell (2008, p. 306), referring to the hero's death in various cultures, argues, "The last act in the biography of the hero is that of the death or departure. Here the whole

Introduction

sense of the life is epitomised. Needless to say, the hero would be no hero if death held for him any terror; the first condition is reconciliation with the grave." Films, which are the products of later cultural eras than the historical epochs Campbell studies, challenge and reshape these old attitudes. In classic films, if a protagonist dies, his death is usually a peaceful event. I do not suggest that a dignified death in films equals a nonviolent death; rather it means dying for morally approved goals from a conservative point of view that a classic film promotes.

Nitobe (2001, p. 5) also writes, "[*Bushido*] is not a written code; at best it consists of a few maxims handed down from the pen of some well-known warrior or savant.... It was an organic growth of decades and centuries of a military career." Related to this idea, Barry D. Steben, in his preface to Yamamoto Tsunetomo's *Hagakure* (the original Japanese text dates to the early 18th century), writes that "*Bushido*—the Way of the Warrior—has long been regarded in Japan as an aesthetic of living, an approach to life that turns living—and dying—into an art" (Tsunetomo, 2008, p. 7). It is not surprising that the warrior mentality is the national attitude in Japanese culture. Historically, the samurai class (*bushi*) was the most important part of the Japanese social pyramid after the shogunate clans. As Tsunetomo (2008) suggests, even during the Tokugawa era (1603–1868), when the country was at peace and samurai were glorified bureaucrats, they still preserved their social prestige and significance. The question here is what precisely this attitude demands from its followers regarding death. The observations of Tsunetomo (2008, p. 25) offer one possible answer to this query: "I have found that *bushido* means to die. It means that when one has to choose between life and death, one just quickly chooses the side of death." He also proposes that death should not be a "dog's death"—that is, dying for an unworthy cause. Honorable death, for a samurai/warrior, means dying while following the orders of the *bakufu* (clan), carrying on his *giri* (obligation/duty), and saving his own or his class's image and reputation. The idea of dying with honor can be juxtaposed with the attitudes toward death exhibited in epic films such as classic Westerns. Similar to the honorific attitude of death among the samurai class, the Western hero has to submit to death willingly and with no fear.

By contrast, Miyamoto Musashi (1584–1645) offers a different attitude toward death, honor, and social status. The philosophy and ideas of Musashi aim to teach the warrior class the moral path to winning battles and living rather than dying. In his lifetime, Musashi fought for many clans (unlike Tsunetomo, who had no war experience). Musashi was also a *ronin* who

Introduction

used his swordsmanship for the benefit of various lords. David K. Groff, in the introduction of *The Five Rings*[4] (2012, p. 7), writes, "Miyamoto Musashi is known in Japan as a *kensei*, a 'sword saint'—a title reserved for those who go so deeply in perfecting the art of swordsmanship that they achieve a deep spiritual enlightenment through it." Although Musashi's teachings are different from Tsunetomo's, he does not suggest cowardice in facing the threat of death. My understanding of Musashi's writings is that he believes that a warrior's focus must be on winning the battle rather than on dying. A clear example of such an attitude can be found in Kurosawa's *Sanjuro* (1962). At one point, the hero is tied to a tree and surrounded by his enemies. Instead of being preoccupied with dying with honor, as Tsunetomo would advocate, he manipulates his enemies to send out a signal that brings a group of young samurai to his rescue.

Furthermore, Musashi has conceptualized dying with honor as a privilege of the general public rather than the province of one specific class. Nitobe (2001) sees honorific death as limited solely to the warrior class because its members have achieved a sense of *giri* (personal honor/duty). However, Musashi (cited in Tsunetomo, 2008, p. 23) argues that anyone who is bound by his/her duty can be privileged with *giri*:

> People usually imagine that the samurai generally thinks about nothing but devoting himself to the way of dying. Yet in the way of dying, there is no distinction between samurai, Buddhist priests, women and the lower classes from the peasants on down. All of them know the principles of gratitude and honor [*giri*], all have a sense of shame, and all are capable of making up their minds to die for these principles. The way of the samurai in the practice of the martial arts is rooted in the resolution to be superior to other people in all things, and it consists in striving to establish one's reputation and position in the world by winning in a single combat or winning in a battle against several people, both for the sake of one's lord and for the sake of oneself. This is all possible through the virtue of the martial arts.

In Kurosawa's works, when a film's character dies with honor, his/her death serves as a social equalizer. Hence Musashi's idea of *giri* is a significant aspect of Kurosawa's heroes. These heroes are concerned with social injustice, death, and honor. Likewise, they do not necessarily belong to the warrior class or a specific historical epoch. An excellent example is the character of Kenji Watanabe (Takashi Shimura) in *Ikiru*. He is neither a samurai nor an army officer. Rather, he is a middle-class bureaucrat living in post–Second World War Tokyo who learns of his impending death from stomach cancer. He does his best to overcome bureaucratic obstacles to build a playground out of a piece of deserted land. His struggle to achieve a positive

Introduction

goal, his sense of ethics and his diligence portray him as a classic film hero. On a cold winter night, he dies peacefully in the playground he has worked so hard to build. This is a clear example of Kurosawa's humanistic attitude—the hero, regardless of the film genre, dies having accomplished his moral goal.

The essence of Kurosawa's heroes is their humanity, sense of duty toward others and response to the different hardships of life and social corruptions. The *ronin* in *Yojimbo* (1961) can be criticized for failing to live by the *bushido* codes. Nonetheless, his attitude is understandable, for the hero, like most people, wants to make a small fortune. We can make the same criticism in the case of Leone's hero in *A Fistful of Dynamite* (1971). On the surface, the hero (a bandit turned revolutionary) is radically different from classic Western heroes. Similar to the *ronin* in *Yojimbo*, he initially engages with the villains to make a fortune. Although his moralities are different from, for example, Ford's heroes, he, like the hero in *Yojimbo*, still undertakes the morally approved deed at the end (in the case of the *Yojimbo*, the hero stands up to the villains, while in Leone's film the hero joins the Mexican revolution).

The Hero's Tragic Death in Film Narrative

The films of Ford, Kurosawa, and Leone include examples of tragic death and incidents, rather than being only tragic tales. Clifford Leech's comparison of epics and tragedy can be linked to this idea. In *Tragedy* (1969, p. 30) he writes, "Where epic and tragedy essentially differ, apart from the fact of performances, is that in epic we have 'tragic moments' in a context which is characterized by amplitude and variety rather than concentration and crisis." Since tragic elements have played a role in many epic tales, from Homer to Tolkien (in literature), and from D.W. Griffith to Peter Jackson (in genre films), the presence of tragedy in the film's story is one of the ordeals that challenge the hero's position. Furthermore, the tragic elements of Leone's and Kurosawa's films are close to the observations of Hegel and Nietzsche. Leech (1969, pp. 22–23) argues that "[t]he 'tragic sense of life'— in Hegel, in Kierkegaard, in Nietzsche … implies … that our situation is necessarily tragic, that all men exist in an evil situation and, if they are aware, are anguished because they are aware." In this rather bleak outlook on life, a film can easily conclude with the hero failing to achieve the idealistic goals of most heroes in classic Western films. Nevertheless, as I will

Introduction

demonstrate in more detail further in this book, no matter how severe the hero's existentialist crisis is, in Kurosawa and Leone films he discovers methods and ways to cope with the aforesaid "tragic sense of life." In short, the point of human life is to live, despite the presence of the forces that aim to extinguish it. The main similarity between the films of Kurosawa and those of Leone is that, for both, human life is sacred. The difference is that Kurosawa shows more examples of social idealism, whereas a sense of cynicism dominates Leone's films.

The first part of Leech's argument is one of the key foundations of Western and samurai films; the tragic death of the hero and its significant impact on the film's conclusion are elements that bring American, Japanese and European films close together. There is no doubt that oriental and occidental art and literature, beyond their similarities, differ regarding the historical, social and cultural concerns on which they reflect. However, an individual's death and its potentially tragic consequences are two areas where the Western films of Ford and Leone are similar to the period films of Kurosawa. Likewise, Kurosawa's westernization (namely, the influence of western visual and written texts on his cinematic vision) brings the idea of tragedy in his films closer to western tragedies.

Leone observes the bleakness of life more as an ironic concept in his films. This does not mean that death and destruction of the innocent are not somber events in his films; as Part Two will demonstrate, through this sense of irony, Leone criticizes unnecessary death rather than ignoring its adverse effect on humanity. As part of this ironic approach to matters of life and death, Leone's heroes respond to the threat of death in unique ways. Leone's heroes, in contrast to Kurosawa's heroes, do not concern themselves with the well-being of others. Rather, Leone's protagonists move forward in a financial sense. They use their mental and physical capabilities to accumulate a fortune; the hero is acquiring a great wealth in tandem with the destruction of the villains. However, this does not mean the termination of the elements that have made the antagonists evil. In Leone's films, even if the hero succeeds, the other characters are not guaranteed to have a less tragic and troubled life beyond the time limit of the storyline. This situation contrasts with Kurosawa's works, where the hero's actions may make life more endurable for others. The exception to this rule is Leone's *A Fistful of Dollars*, which is a direct remake (with two additional scenes—the shooting in the cemetery, and the massacre of the soldiers on the riverbank) of Kurosawa's *Yojimbo*.

The next point is that tragic Greek plays have influenced the Western

Introduction

film genre as well. Pantelis Michelakis, in *Greek Tragedy on Screen* (2013, p. 132), refers to this influence: "Greek tragedy, helps the legitimization of the western as a film genre, the valorization of film genres as worthy descendants or competitors of classical literary genres, and finally the sanction of the myth of the genre as a fixed and pure category with essential qualities." Furthermore, Michelakis, referring to Laurence Giavarini's arguments, suggests some aspects of this influence: "The [W]estern, like tragedy, belonged to a specific space and time[;] it was about the frontier, which is nothing other than a transformation of the boundary, and of a particular savage state in humans" (2013, p. 133). This frontier could recall Mackey-Kallis' idea of the wasteland, given that the hero, in his journey and through his actions, transforms the wasteland/frontier.

In addition, John Simons, in *Peckinpah's Tragic Westerns* (2011), argues that the revenge elements of the Christian tragedy have a strong presence in classic Westerns as well. The focus of this type of tragedy is on the hero's revenge against the villains that have mistreated him. Simons (2011, p. 22) defines this concept as "Christian tragedy ... [with an] emphasis on heroic sacrifice and the effects of such sacrifice on the fallen world the hero occupies and to some extent redeems." The idea of the Christian tragedy relates to the notion mentioned above regarding "balance." That is, throughout the narrative, the villains will challenge and, at times, hurt the good and virtuous, just as the villainous Clanton family kills two of Wyatt Earp's brothers in Ford's *My Darling Clementine*; by the end of the film, the hero responds to this challenge by killing the villains.

Despite the influence that western art and literature had on several aspects of Kurosawa's films, including their tragic elements, he nevertheless made films within the Japanese studio system (which, as explained earlier, allows directors more artistic freedom than directors in Hollywood). Kurosawa, in his autobiography (1983), refers to the influence of the tragic elements of Shakespeare's plays and Dostoevsky's novels on his own mentality. Time and location separated these two writers, but there are similarities between their works. Both writers deal with heroes who live in a tragic world but seek to improve the world around them by challenging what they consider its demons. Steiner (1961, p. 16), writing about the Elizabethan plays, can relate to the effects of Shakespearian dialogue in Kurosawa's vision: "In Elizabethan theatre, the idea of tragedy lost its medieval directness ... the sense of [tragedy] reached beyond the fall of individual greatness.... The sense of life is itself shadowed by a feeling of tragedy." These same ideas apply to many of Kurosawa's heroes, as he shows them

Introduction

tangled in situations where political, social and personal evils (such as war, political turmoil or physical and psychological illness) overshadow law, humanity, and virtues. It is part of the hero's mission to challenge such evils. In addition, Kurosawa's hero is not necessarily concerned with personal glory and survival. That is why he often attempts to understand and better the lives of others.

The methods through which the threat of death can enlighten and motivate an individual differ among the heroes portrayed by Ford, Kurosawa, and Leone, as will be explored later in this book. However, the current section is focused on common ground. The question is how this education, related to death and the tragic moments of the films, contributes to the hero's discovery of his abilities. Campbell argues that there are hidden powers and skills in all human beings. An individual evolves to become a hero as he realizes his previously undiscovered powers during his life journey. Campbell (2008, pp. 204–205) states, "The individual, through prolonged psychological disciplines, gives up completely all attachment to his personal limitations, idiosyncrasies, hopes, and fears, no longer resists the self-annihilation that is prerequisite to rebirth in the realization of truth … [and] becomes, that is to say, an anonymity." This can mean that a tragic incident, such as the death of the hero's loved ones, functions as a psychological ordeal that tests an individual's mental and physical abilities. Sir Philip Sidney's concept of the "Golden World" in poetry can be linked to the latter point. Leech (1969, p. 33), in his interpretations of Sidney's Golden World, argues that the Golden World "is not a world where everything is good, but a world where things exist in a pure rather than a mixed form. What is important is the sense of full, or at least unusual, the realization of the powers and tendencies peculiar to man. Orestes kills his mother, Oedipus marries his mother and kills his father, Medea kills her children: yet they are, in a sense, more fully themselves than men and women usually dare to be." These morbid and somehow cruel comments illustrate the existentialist character of some well-known heroes. I reason, however, that the hero's "realization of the powers and tendencies peculiar to man" is the aspect of Sidney's ideas that can be linked to films and the effects of tragedy on the hero's position in the story.

Therefore, these tragic occurrences can be opportunities that motivate an ordinary man, in overcoming his fears and insecurities, to relate to his inner powers and become a hero. This situation also applies to action-based and historical films, where, in most cases, the hero, overwhelmed by life tragedies, begins a journey (Campbell calls this the "call of adventure") in

Introduction

which he will discover/rediscover his emotional and physical strength. Once the hero successfully overcomes threats of death, he gains the ability to function as a symbol for all humankind (or at least the film audience). The writings of Leech and Dorothea Krook on the tragic hero in literature can be linked to my ideas. The former says, "The tragic hero ... is 'one of us.' He is not necessarily virtuous, not necessarily free from profound guilt. What he is is a man who reminds us strongly of our own humanity, who can be accepted as standing for us" (Leech, 1969, p. 46). Krook's ideas suggest a similar principle; she points out that the hero "is represented in a special sense. He is all mankind: representative of all humanity in embodying some fundamental, persistent aspect of man's nature.... In showing in his suffering and his knowledge the necessary common ground with his fellow creatures to make these truly exemplary and instructive" (Krook, 1969, pp. 36–37). These ideas are applicable to those heroes of Ford, Kurosawa, and Leone that are directly involved in the process of unifying a nation. However, Leech and Krook focus on how tragedies are concerned with how to be human, whereas Ford, Kurosawa, and Leone demonstrate how to be a human being while dealing with the significant political, social and economic changes that occur in their respective societies. In addition, in these films, the hero's shortcomings are part of their humanity. The archetypal hero's encounter with death/the threat of death (and his response to the tragedy/potential tragedy element of death) shows the depth of his moral concern for the good of humanity.

I apply Campbell's theory regarding the archetypal hero, and his connection to the theme of death, to this book's discussions. Although heroes in diverse cultural/social/cinematic settings can be similar, according to the genre conventions that govern these characters and their social/historical contextualization, they evolve into complex individuals that enrich the films of Ford, Kurosawa, and Leone. This is where the theme of death performs a pivotal role. The hero's death, or his survival of the threat of death, influences the narrative in various directions.

The main body of *The Hero and the Grave: The Theme of Death in the Films of John Ford, Akira Kurosawa and Sergio Leone* includes four parts. The first part, "Fundamental Functions of Death Within the Narrative," studies the attitudes of Ford, Kurosawa, and Leone toward conventional heterosexual romance. This section will further explain the characteristics of the two major subthemes of the theme of death—the cycle of life and the cult of death—in the films of these directors. I will also study how these two concepts can function as fundamental strategies to advance the plot in

Introduction

the films of Ford, Kurosawa, and Leone. In this section, I shall offer a close reading of death in Ford's *Stagecoach* (1939) and *My Darling Clementine* (1946); Kurosawa's *Rashomon* (1950); and Leone's *A Fistful of Dollars* (1964). The reason for choosing films as case studies in this and subsequent parts of the book is that, together, they will offer a rich and unexplained ground for comparative analysis of the works of these three directors based on the theme of death.

In Parts Two, Three and Four, I shall consider the variations of death in works of Ford, Kurosawa, and Leone. These variations are death in battle, suicide and natural death. In these sections, I will study the representation and the functions of the cycle of life and the cult of death in the case of each type of death. Additionally, I will study how each of the previously mentioned types of death affects the hero's position in the films.

The second part, "The Hero's Position and the Theme of Death in Battle," tackles the complicated relationship between the theme of death in battle and the cycle of life/cult of death as represented in a film's conclusion. These issues will be the center of my close analysis of Ford's *Fort Apache* (1948); Kurosawa's *Kagemusha* (1980); and Leone's *The Good, the Bad and the Ugly* (1966) and *Once Upon a Time in the West* (1968).

The third part, "Narrative Attitude Toward the Hero's Suicide," argues that the hero's suicide can leave two ideological marks on a film. First, suicide redeems the hero/anti-hero from their past life as long as this past, according to generic codes of Western or *jidaigeki* films, is morally stigmatized. Second, an act of self-destruction portrays the despairing mentality that a character (usually a minor character) endures. These two types of suicide shape and influence the relationship between the hero and the cycle of life and cult of death. The case studies for this section include Ford's *3 Godfathers* (1948) and *7 Women* (1967); Kurosawa's *Red Beard* (1965); and Leone's *For a Few Dollars More* (1965) and *A Fistful of Dynamite* (1971).

The last part, "The Hero's Natural Death: Narrating the Past and the Way of the Future," classifies and observes the similarities and differences between the approaches of Ford, Kurosawa, and Leone regarding natural death in their films. This section will (a) compare Ford and Kurosawa's attitudes toward death due to illness, and (b) explain the general implications of a lack of natural death in Leone's films. The analyses of the fourth section will mainly be concerned with Ford's *The Man Who Shot Liberty Valance* (1962); Kurosawa's *Red Beard*; and Leone's *Once Upon a Time in the West*.

Part One

Fundamental Functions of Death Within the Narrative

1

Romantic Involvement and Redemption

As part of the Western genre epistemology and, indeed, most visual and literary traditions, romantic attachment to women challenges the male hero's initial position in the narrative. Additionally, in certain cases, romance serves as one aspect of the atonement of a criminal or an antihero from his previous behavior and misdeeds, as is the case with Ringo (John Wayne) in Ford's *Stagecoach* (1939). At other times, the hero does not form a permanent union with a woman, instead having a short-lived platonic relationship with her, as is the case in *Shane* (1953, dir. George Stevens).

To understand the position of love in films and its relation to the theme of death, I will study the basic ideas of romance. Rewarding the hero with romantic attachment is a common theme in most ancient cultures and myths. Campbell (2008, p. 91) calls this situation the "ultimate adventure" of the hero: "The ultimate adventure, when all the barriers and ogres [of the male hero's id] have been overcome, is commonly represented as a mystical marriage of the triumphant hero-soul with the Queen Goddess of the world. This is the crisis at the nadir, at the zenith, or at the uttermost edge of the temple, or in the darkness of the deepest chamber of the heart." Put more simply, once the hero successfully defeats his enemies, he will marry his love interest. Since the hero represents the inner goodness of mankind, his enemies represent what is wrong with mankind, and marriage with his beloved connects the hero to all that is good and morally pure. Likewise, Northrop Frye, in *Anatomy of Criticism* (1973, p. 186), observes the presence of the theme of romantic love in written texts as a way of encoding bigger ideological concerns: "In every age, the ruling social or intellectual class tends to project its ideals in some form of romance, where the virtuous heroes and beautiful heroines represent the ideals and the villains the threats to their ascendancy."

1. Romantic Involvement and Redemption

These arguments on the ideology of love in the written western text and its effects on the hero's journey are similar to the Western genre conventions. The storytelling tradition to which Western heroes are assigned is one that Wexman, in Richard Neupert's *The End: Narration and Closer in the Cinema* (1995, p. 44), calls "dynastic nostalgia." This conventional happy ending includes one or more of the following elements: the death of the villain(s), the hero's emotional involvement with a wife/sweetheart and the hero's discovery of a new home/state of mind. As a result, the newly forged family enhances the value of the ethics and morals that the actions of the villain were defiling during the film.

The above structure is readily perceived in the case of Ford's *Stagecoach*. Ringo's initial goal is avenging the deaths of his father and brother, murdered by the Plummer boys. He encounters Dallas on his journey of revenge, falls in love with her and asks her to marry him. However, involvement with Dallas does not alter Ringo's goal of confronting his rivals. He has no legal duty to encounter his family's murderers; nevertheless, he has the same generic obligation that classic heroes usually have: to fulfill their moral responsibility. Hagin (2010, p. 17) speaks about the morality of the victorious heroes in classic Westerns: "The victor in the shootout ... is not the most skillful (although sometimes nothing contradicts this), but the one who has followed the correct path and was the most 'moral.'" In the case of Ringo, his moral goal/duty is to avenge his family. He faces their killers in a standoff and kills them. Thus he has fulfilled his quest, and the villains have paid for their crimes.

The question is how the romantic attachment to a woman relates to the theme of death. Buscombe (1992, p. 59) writes, "Women in the Western represent the alternative to violence. Characteristically, the hero is faced with a choice: either he follows his code, which demands that he face physical danger and meet evil with force, or he chooses romance. What the woman offers is always the easy way out." The idea of a hero facing two options is often accurate, but the hero usually ends up with both in the end (e.g., *High Noon* [1952]). A hero often meets his love interest when he is pursuing other goals. The effect of this encounter is that if the hero does not have an entirely moral past, like Ringo, he has now a chance for a moral life. This view slightly contradicts Buscombe's conclusion, for it argues that romantic involvement does not necessarily mean a way out of generic codes and goals. In classic genres such as the Western, the protagonist can be in love and still pursue his goal, assuming that it is a moral one and will contribute to the civic progress of the society.

Part One—Fundamental Functions of Death Within the Narrative

The hero's union with the woman he loves becomes possible only after standing up to the villains. In classic Westerns, potential marriage with such a woman is one of the leading foundations of an ethical and civilized society, and thus her presence is necessary for the historical transformations of the American nation. Andre Bazin (2009, p. 155), in his seminal work *What Is Cinema?*, writes on this matter, "The myth of the western illustrates, and both initiates and confirms woman in her role as vestal of the social virtues, of which the chaotic world is so greatly in need. Within her is concealed the physical future, and by way of the institution of the family to which she aspires as the root is drawn to the earth, its mortal foundation." In the case of *Stagecoach*, instead of being free from any legal and moral commitment, Ringo adopts what is unknown and alien to him: a potential family and settled life.

I also suggest that in Ford's films, the leading hero can be redeemed from his past conduct when he is about to reach or when he tries to achieve his goals. This redemption occurs at several levels and thus changes the hero's position in multiple directions. Consider the case of Ringo. The first time he is introduced to the audience, he is a young single man and a fugitive from the law, and his primary goal is avenging the deaths of his father and brother. By the film's conclusion, in addition to killing the Plummer boys, he has traveled through the wasteland that is the desert, encountered Indians, fought them victoriously and contributed to saving the lives of the passengers of the stagecoach; he has also, after confessing his love for Dallas, asked her to marry him and received her consent. So, on the way to reach his initial goal (seeking revenge), he is given two more goals—namely, fighting the Indians and establishing a morally sanctioned partnership with the woman he loves. At the end of the film, Ringo informs Dallas that he should serve his prison sentence before marrying her. However, the marshal (who serves as the film's agent for promoting moral and traditional romance) permits Ringo to abscond with Dallas, though in doing so he departs from his role as the protector of the law. Regardless, Ringo's earlier decision proves that he has reached the civilized maturity through which law and order must be preserved, even if this means he must return to prison.

Moreover, since Dallas is single, her involvement with Ringo poses no moral obstacles. As part of the film's conclusion, they travel toward his farm, an indication that they will create a family together. Ringo's character transitions from a fugitive to a law-abiding person who respects legal judgments, from a lone avenger to a protector who defends the innocent, and from an uninvolved bachelor to a potential husband.

In some cases, the death of the Ford's supporting heroes (like Hatfield

1. Romantic Involvement and Redemption

in *Stagecoach*) marks their redemption. Hatfield is redeemed on one level only: he goes from being a gambler to a martyr. This could be because he is a supporting hero in the film, and his role carries less archetypal significance than the main lead. Hatfield's only goal is to save Mrs. Mallory from the attack of the Indians. Hatfield does not have a marriage quest, due primarily to Hollywood's traditional approach to love. His involvement with Mrs. Mallory does not result in sexual union, for she is a married woman. Hence, Ford portrays Hatfield as the type of hero who is acting according to the dictates of conventional morality, for he never makes any advances toward Mrs. Mallory.

Hatfield's death, beyond symbolizing the defeated Southern aristocratic society, has a redemptive quality. Although he dies in the process of saving Mrs. Mallory, he reconnects with his roots as a Southern aristocrat who helps those who are in the same social class as himself. Therefore, he mentions his father just before he dies; Hatfield, at the hour of his death, is reaching his birth identity. His death informs the audience of his past story. Hagin (2010, pp. 12–13) notes that "in classical Hollywood films, death can bring about a shift from ignorance to knowledge. It can be a discovery of new information or the disclosure of a secret." By giving this information to the audience, Ford clarifies Hatfield's backstory; this untold story is what Bordwell et al. call "retardation," defined as follows: "Every [plot] uses retardation to postpone complete construction of the [story]. At the very least, the end of the story, or the means whereby we arrive there, will be withheld" (1985, p. 52). Therefore, Hatfield's death also functions to encompass the story, or at least his portion of the story in the film.

Concepts of love and redemption work well in the case of Ford's Westerns since the genre codes have established romance as part of the narrative, whereas romance is usually absent from Japanese period films, including those of Kurosawa, who admits in Cardullo (2008, p. 6) that "[w]omen simply aren't my speciality." The romantic attachment between the hero and his love interest in Kurosawa's samurai films does not have the same redemptive quality of Ford's Western films. This may be one reason why women do not have the same ideological significance in Kurosawa's films compared to Ford's works. However, now and then, as is the case with *Sanjuro*, Kurosawa's male heroes encounter women who educate them on how to be a mature and caring human being, but the hero cannot be romantically involved with these women because of their old age or their class status (they are nobles whereas the hero is from the warrior class). In other cases, like *Rashomon*, corrupt sexual attraction replaces romance.

Part One—Fundamental Functions of Death Within the Narrative

Despite the general lack of sexual love in Kurosawa's films, romance (similar to Ford's films) is at times part of his films' narrative structure. In these rare cases, Kurosawa, on the surface, follows the conventions of a typical romantic story. On this point, Mellen (2002, p. 13) writes, "[In *Seven Samurai*] Katsushiro's passion for farmer Manzo's daughter, Shino (Keiko Tsushima), contains the universal defiance of young love, a passion which transcends class, history, time or expectation." However, the outcome of this romance is different from Ford's approach to love in his films. In *Seven Samurai*, Katsushiro relinquishes his love for the village girl and, as a result, returns to his generic obligations. It should be said that, as Prince has suggested, during the 16th century (when the story of *Seven Samurai* is set), the samurai class was not separated from farming communities; thus the love story could have worked. However, I argue that Kurosawa is engaged with an approach from the Edo era regarding this romance since that class culture is better known to the audience. If Katsushiro's relationship with the village girl had evolved, he would have stayed in the village with his beloved and followed his wishes (*ninjo*) rather than becoming a samurai and following his sense of *giri* (duty).

Before I analyze the effects of the lack of romance on the *Rashomon* narrative, it is necessary to provide a summary of the film's story, as the narrative of *Rashomon* is a complex one. *Rashomon* begins with the meeting of a woodcutter (Takashi Shimura), a Buddhist priest (Minoru Chiaki) and a commoner (Kichijiro Ueda) amid the ruins of a Buddhist temple. While the three men are taking shelter from the rain, the woodcutter and the priest recall the events of a trial they attended earlier that day. Their story follows the accounts of four eyewitnesses to the murder of a samurai—a bandit, the samurai's wife, a medium connected to the dead samurai's spirit, and the woodcutter; each witness's story differs from the next. The bandit Tajōmaru (Toshiro Mifune) confesses to raping the samurai's wife (Machiko Kyō) and then killing the warrior (Masayuki Mori). The samurai's wife, however, pleads guilty to killing her husband, whereas the spirit (as conveyed by the medium) admits that the samurai killed himself. Lastly, the woodcutter says that the bandit murdered the samurai in a very gritty manner.

In Kurosawa's *Rashomon*, a samurai, who is the symbol of ethics and authority, behaves in a manner that goes against the rules of *bushi*. These actions contrast with Ford's approach to archetypes of the Western genre and relate significantly to Leone's attitude toward those same archetypes, as the cowboys in Leone's films do not act according to the classic Western's codes of conduct.

1. Romantic Involvement and Redemption

Rashomon shows the warrior to be an individual who, in contrast to the ethics of the samurai class, is seeking financial fortune. His lack of respect for conservative rules of his social class overtakes his wife as well: Kurosawa positions the warrior's wife as a character who does not follow the ethical norms of the time that this film portrays. Either a victim of sexual assault or a partner in her husband's death, she is associated with sexual deprivation. The corrupt attitudes of these characters reflect the historical period that the film covers. Prince (1991, p. 128) argues that the historical era that is the setting for this film (the 12th century) "seemed to be the period known in Buddhist prophecy as 'the end of the law' when human life would fall to its point of greatest degeneracy." I argue that the undignified death of a samurai and the impossibility of knowing the truth behind his demise are the ways through which Kurosawa depicts this era.

Among the film's characters, only the Buddhist priest appears to be decent. However, he, too, has his doubts about the teachings of Buddha. By the end of the film, however, his faith is restored when the woodcutter adopts an abandoned newborn baby. This infant is a symbol of the innocence and purity that the adults lack. By adopting the baby, the woodcutter takes his first step toward achieving this purity (even if he is not conscious of it). The adoption also explains the evolution of the priest's character in the story. The priest initially represents the lack of trust in the goodness of men. Witnessing the incident brought to the court and becoming involved with the legal procedures of the case has gradually made him a cynic. James Goodwin, in *Akira Kurosawa and Intertextual Cinema* (1994, p. 137), writes, "The priest ... serves a role similar to the *waki no shite* (side doer) in Noh theatre. The *waki* reflects the thoughts, emotions, and motives of the main figure, or *shite*, though he typically remains a commentator rather than an agent in the play's action." This is one of the priest's roles: he is an outside observer who speaks about the dearth of decency among human beings. At first, he has a very general view of this lack and does not express any thoughts on people's ability to be moral beings. Nonetheless, his mentality changes when the woodcutter adopts the baby. The priest praises the woodcutter's action, for it has restored his hope in humanity.

Additionally, the troubled woodcutter in *Rashomon*, as Goodwin (1994) puts it, realizes that he has a new choice in life as he gets involved with society. Initially, he removes himself from the community—that is, he conceals the truth about the samurai's death from the court. His position changes when he becomes the guardian of the newborn baby. The woodcutter's attitude and conduct can be related to Thornton's idea of the social hero, even though he is not a high-ranking official. Thus, it can be said that, although not a warrior, the woodcutter does something for the future of society. The significant point here is that Kurosawa suggests that an individual does not need to belong to the warrior class to take moral actions. Hence, the adoption storyline means that the woodcutter has begun to take notice of other choices in his life.

Leone's films, similar to most European Westerns and Japanese period films, pay little attention to romance. Nor are his films concerned with the cycle of life and starting a family. Leone concentrates more on themes like the extensive moral decay of society, male friendship, and personal survival. This explains why the female characters of his films (especially within the *Dollar* trilogy) are not integrated into a thriving community.

The lack of romance can explain the main hero's emotional and physical avoidance of women in Leone's *A Fistful of Dollars*, which is a remake of Akira Kurosawa's *Yojimbo*. Leone's film is what Harvey Roy Greenberg, in Constantine Verevis' *Film Remakes* (2006, p. 9), calls "the unacknowledged, disguised remake"—that is, "minor or major alterations (in character, time and setting) are undertaken, but the audience is not informed of the original film version." Besides, as Verevis explains (2006, p. 88), "just as Kurosawa had reworked the conventions of the [Japanese period film] with a revolutionary approach to swordplay, music and sound effects, Leone transformed the conditions of the European Western, introducing a new kind of realism and a hero who was negative, dirty, who looked like a human being, and who was totally at home with the violence which surrounded him."

The lack of romance affects the relationship between the theme of death and the hero's redemption from his past actions. To understand this point, first, we need to know how the lack of romance is justified in Leone's Westerns. In his films, Leone does not provide the hero with a moral/ethical role model. This means that there is no one to encourage the hero to seek a settled family life. In these works, figures of law and order are either unethical (part of criminal organizations) or morally weak (incapable of challenging the established corrupt morality of the community/society in which they live). In *A Fistful of Dollars*, Baxter is a sheriff and a settled, married man. He is also a criminal. Legally and morally, his hypocrisy cannot offer a role model for the hero. This contrasts with Ford's films, in which, when there is a love story in the plot, there is also a figure of law and paternal authority that encourages this love (e.g., Marshal Wilcox in *Stagecoach*). This arrangement may be due to Hollywood's traditional pres-

1. Romantic Involvement and Redemption

entation of sheriffs as ethical and moral individuals, which gives weight to their validation of the hero's romantic interests. In addition, as Hagin (2010) contextualizes, the Hollywood filmmaking guidebooks emphasized the goodness of law figures.

The female characters of Leone's *For a Few Dollars More* and *The Good, the Bad and the Ugly*, in their short time on screen, do not undergo any of the changes that women in Ford's Westerns would experience. These changes, in Ford's movies, suggest that female characters follow the approved morality of a conservative western society. It also means that, by becoming the love interest of a hero, they can affect the hero's position in relation to death. In contrast, since Leone's films are more about the individual's survival, women often do not challenge the hero's position in the story. For example, in *The Good, the Bad and the Ugly* the first unnamed female character to appear (Chelo Alonso) witnesses the murder of her husband and older son by Angel Eyes (Lee Van Cleef). She faints following the tragedy, and the audience does not see her character again. Later, the prostitute Maria (Rada Rassimov) is beaten by Angel Eyes, but this incident does not motivate her to take any action against him. She does not represent the redeemable prostitute that Western films such as Ford's *Stagecoach* portray.

In his *Dollar* trilogy Leone illustrates a universe that is similar to the classic samurai films, in which the masculinity and narcissism of male heroes beget no emotional or sexual connection with women. Kitses (2004, p. 256) writes on this matter, "The absence of women is the most telling comment on the world depicted in the *Dollar* trilogy. Leone's avowed interest was in an epic cinema, the province of which 'by definition, is a masculine universe.'" As Leone confessed in his interview with Christopher Frayling (2008), his male heroes are not romantic. Instead, they see women as a nuisance interfering with their primary goal of surviving the corrupt environment in which they live. This high degree of individualism means that Leone's heroes are not concerned with forming groups like a family or community.

Hitherto I have argued that the lack of a moral role model can establish the hero's lack of interest in romance. However, the absence of traditional romance does not mean a lack of redemption or a near-death experience, though the representation of redemption in Leone's *Dollar* trilogy is different from Ford's take on the same concept. In *A Fistful of Dollars*, the anonymous hero's assistance to Marisol and her family shows that he has a sense of morality that motivates him to do what is right. Furthermore, by

Part One—Fundamental Functions of Death Within the Narrative

assigning the hero this secondary function and goal, Leone portrays the hero's courage in a critical situation. By helping a hapless woman even when he is not in love with her (or, indeed, related to her), the hero compensates for his previous unethical actions.

The hero's initial goal of chasing a fortune is a common trait in European Westerns. Alberto Moravia, in Frayling's *Sergio Leone: Something to Do with Death* (2000, p. 118), explains this code: "[In European Westerns t]he dominant theme is no longer the struggle between the lone, intrepid individual and the negative forces of nature and society: the dominant theme is the scramble for money." However, this desire for financial gain does not mean that the hero will not become involved in doing the right thing. In fact, in Leone's films, a significant aspect of hero's rite of passage is that he gets involved with other people's lives and helps them, even if this means facing the threat of death.

At one point, the hero of *A Fistful of Dollars* informs Marisol of his reason for saving her: "I knew someone like you who no one helped." Leone avoids telling the audience why the hero did not help this absent character or who she was. The crucial point is that the fate of this unknown character has affected the hero's motivation.

In *A Fistful of Dollars*, the hero, after helping Marisol, has a near-death experience when he is brutally beaten and tortured by Ramon Rojo and his men. Frayling (2000) and Kitses (2004) have argued that the hero's torture and near-death experience are a secular version of Jesus' crucifixion; both heroes are beaten savagely, and both born anew. I suggest that this experience is Leone's way of signifying the hero's physical redemption. Once he survives the threat of death, in the film's finale, he faces the Rojo clan and kills them all to save his innkeeper friend from their abuse and torture. So, it can be argued that surviving the threat of death compels the hero to take moral actions.

2

The Cycle of Life

The idea of rebirth alters the hero's initial position in the films of Ford, Kurosawa, and Leone. However, since these directors are from diverse cultural and historical backgrounds, there are some variations in their respective takes on this concept. I have identified the following functions for the cycle of life: (a) transcending the tragic nature of the hero/moral person's death; (b) continuity of life, and thus of the human race; (c) the rediscovery of once-possessed moral values and attitudes in an individual who is involved directly or indirectly with the cycle of life (either as a parent or as a guardian of a newborn baby); and (d) compensation for the destruction of the life of a dead friend/beloved—that is, the life of a newborn baby replaces the life that has been lost.

There are two strategies for showing the hero's attitude to the cycle of life. First, what I call the "favorable" attitude is seen when a character (usually the hero) either forms a family or tries to do so. The second attitude is what I call "avoidance." This scenario occurs when the hero circumvents forming a traditional family, whether deliberately or accidentally. In Ford's films, the birth of a new baby (which can happen in the middle of a crisis such as fighting villains) most likely implies the promise of a more civilized and prosperous future for the American people. In this situation, the American society is freed from those evil actions that threaten its safety. In Kurosawa's films, the presence of a newborn baby, and indeed a young child in the plot, suggests the possibility of change in a society/community that is overwhelmed by death and moral decay. However, this change is more on an individualistic level and does not necessarily mean a better and more civilized future for the entire community. In Leone's films the social ethics are lacking, which means that children usually share the same deadly ordeals as the adults; in some cases, children do not even survive the threat of death.

The preexisting concept of the cycle of life in the ancient texts involves both the birth of a child and the birth of a new mentality in an individual.

Part One—Fundamental Functions of Death Within the Narrative

The latter option relates to the hero's romantic attachment to a woman and how the hero's personality matures during this process. Campbell (2008, p. 16) explains the relationship between birth and death as one of the functions of the cycle of life in ancient epic tales: "Only birth can conquer death—the birth, not of the old thing again, but of something new. Within the soul, within the body social, there must be—if we are to experience long survival—a continuous 'recurrence of birth' (*palingenesia*) to nullify the unremitting recurrences of death." Campbell here emphasizes the importance of moral and physical rebirth for mankind's survival. In keeping with Campbell's argument, I suggest that the idea of birth compensating for the death of individuals is a common theme in films of diverse cultural backgrounds. Likewise, there are similarities as well as differences in the cultural and cinematic attitudes of Ford, Kurosawa, and Leone regarding this idea.

In Ford's films, women evolve into socially active (within a traditional setting) and responsible individuals (in a conservative sense) who maintain the previously mentioned balance between life and death. In keeping this balance, they contribute to the civic progress of society, not only out of cinematic convention or social expectation but also out of moral conviction. In the classical Hollywood films, there are usually two types of motherhood: the physical/biological mother and the caring/nurturing mother. Mrs. Mallory (Louise Platt) of *Stagecoach* falls into the former category, whereas Dallas is the latter type.

The first type of motherhood sees women only as a "womb" that can give birth. The second category extends to a woman's nurturing abilities after the birth of her child. *Stagecoach* is mainly concerned with the second type of motherhood. Although Dallas has nurturing abilities, being a prostitute casts a moral shadow on her potential role as a mother. At the beginning of the film, older married women, who represent conservative values, have expelled her from the town. They all dress in head-to-toe grey-colored garments and walk next to each other as a single entity that suggests matrimony and years of settled life. Dallas' vocation has defined her as a morally compromised person. Even if she cares for the well-being of others, the old women do not recognize her as someone who is capable of being decent and undertaking positive deeds. For them, Dallas' social position is definite, and they force her to leave town. The exile scene is the first time that Ford portrays her as an outsider from the spectrum of moral values of the larger group. The second time is during the lunch scene, in which all the stagecoach passengers (except for Ringo, who recognizes her as a fellow outcast) ignore her. During Mrs. Mallory's labor, however, Ford illustrates the trans-

2. The Cycle of Life

formation of Dallas from prostitute to a surrogate mother. She is the one who takes the infant from the biological mother and holds it in her arms. The scene in which all the male passengers of the stagecoach come together to see the newborn baby is crucial. They are not just excited to see a baby; they are also gathering to celebrate Dallas' newfound maternal ability. Joseph McBride (2003, p. 286) reflects on this very scene, "As Dallas holds the child for others to see ... Ford transforms Dallas with radiant lighting, revealing her inner goodness." The care that Dallas provides for the child does not refer solely to her motherly instinct; it also points out her new position in the film—she is a nurturing and caring surrogate mother who can also be a decent and moral individual.

Although Ford does not explicitly indicate that Ringo and Dallas will have children, the ideological conventions of classical Hollywood (in addition to specific narrative nuances in the film) suggest that they will. Ringo is encouraged to ask for Dallas' hand after the birth of Mrs. Mallory's baby as he realizes that Dallas is the one. The film's script emphasizes this point through a line of dialogue, where Ringo informs Dallas of when "I saw you carrying that baby." This begins a conversation that leads to a marriage proposal. Similarly, their potential marriage indicates that both can be moral, law-abiding citizens. By becoming a wife and adapting to the ethical roles of a traditional settled woman, Dallas is no longer a prostitute. Nonprocreative, casual and stigmatized sexual encounters are replaced with marital and traditionally sanctioned sex that may ultimately lead to a family. Ringo's attitude toward the cycle of life is what I have identified as favorable in that he adapts to a new role as an involved man. Once he has avenged his father's and brother's deaths at the film's conclusion, he can raise an archetypal family with a woman he loves. This is a sign that he is no longer a criminal. This style of conclusion is common among classic Hollywood films. Bordwell's writings in *Narration in the Fiction Film* (1986, p. 16) elaborate on this point: "Hollywood characters, especially protagonists, are goal-oriented. The hero desires something new in regard to his/her situation, or the hero seeks to restore an original state of affairs." So, if Ringo's goal is to kill the Plummer boys and marry Dallas, by the film's conclusion he has achieved these goals.

The love storyline of *Stagecoach* means that Dallas' unsettled lifestyle, which differs from the lifestyle of the women who condemned her to exile, will end. Although being a caring/surrogate mother prepares Dallas for motherhood, there is still a degree of distinction between the biological and caring mother in this film. However, in his other films, Ford combines

Part One—Fundamental Functions of Death Within the Narrative

both attitudes toward motherhood. (I will scrutinize the result of this combination in Part Two.)

During the famous chase scene in the film (the Indians attacking the stagecoach), amid all the mayhem of the battle, it is Dallas who watches over the newborn baby while Mrs. Mallory is too scared to take any action, including taking care of her child. Therefore, Ford contextualizes Dallas' bravery and caring skills as a paradigm. In Ford's later films, this paradigm evolves, and the concept of the caring mother becomes a prominent aspect of his films. For example, in *My Darling Clementine*, Clementine (Cathy Downs) stays in Tombstone and becomes the teacher for the children in the community. The army wives of Ford's cavalry trilogy likewise become caring mothers for the platoons that expand the west and try to better the future of their nation.

In *Stagecoach*, Mrs. Mallory represents an army wife. Her marriage to a cavalryman suggests that she has adopted the traditional role of a wife and mother. Therefore, from a conventional point of view, she is a decent individual. Furthermore, the status of her husband is quite significant. His position in the army means that, as part of his vocation, he is facing the threat of death while trying to expand the frontier. At the end of the chase, the miraculous arrival of the cavalry forces the Indians to retreat. The army has thus replaced the individual, as it has adopted the protective role of the husband and father for Mrs. Mallory and her child, respectively. Thus, the survival of Mrs. Mallory means the perseverance of the traditional view on family life.

In contrast to *Stagecoach*, Ford's *My Darling Clementine* features an example of the male hero's (Doc Holliday) "avoidance" of the cycle of life. In the light of conventional Christian and Hollywood traditions, Doc Holliday (Victor Mature) is a morally compromised person. Though his fiancée, Clementine, is a decent and educated young woman, he lives out of wedlock with a saloon girl, Chihuahua (Linda Darnell). Nevertheless, Ford portrays traces of the traditional morality in Holliday's character. He throws a cheating gambler out of town, and, when necessary, even if he is motivated to avenge his mistress's death, he helps the figures of law (namely, Wyatt Earp and his brother).

Holliday suffers from tuberculosis and is in a critical condition. His inability to help himself despite his status as a doctor has made him a cynical and depressed alcoholic. His way of life, however, is not enough to bring him to the level of morally compromised people like the Clanton family. To be genuinely corrupt, he would have to become a villain who kills innocent people unjustly. This transition is the most crucial aspect of growing evil in any classic Hollywood film. Holliday does not go through such a transition.

The next question is that, if at the end Holliday fights alongside the law, why should he die in the gunfight? In reality, Doc Holliday died of tuberculosis six years after the shootout at the OK Corral, which took place on October 26, 1881, in Tombstone, Arizona. However, considering that Holliday is an important supporting character in a Western film, his violent death while fighting against the villains matches the moral concerns of the genre. In addition, his death clears the way for the union of Wyatt and Clementine. If, for example, Holliday did not die, then Wyatt could have no chance of winning Clementine's affections by the film's conclusion. Besides, Holliday's violent death in the film is his punishment for his moral failings in life.

Earlier I wrote that romantic involvement with a woman could redeem a morally flawed film character. If this is so, why does Holliday's relationship with Chihuahua not lead to redemption? The answer is that Holliday's sexual relationship with Chihuahua does not rise to a romantic one that can form a cycle of life. Likewise, Chihuahua's position as a fallen woman in this film is ossified. Ford offers no tangible sign that Holliday genuinely loves her (in contrast to *Stagecoach*, where we can be sure that Ringo's love for Dallas is real). Moreover, although Holliday appears to depend emotionally on Chihuahua at the beginning of the film, through the narrative he gradually loses his interest in her. The signs are vivid and abundant— he does not say that he loves her, he leaves for Mexico without her despite promising to take her with him, and he is emotionally cold and stiff when Chihuahua kisses him.

Holliday's lack of romantic feelings for his mistress can be justified in that she is the third person in his relationship with Clementine. Chihuahua's vocation, therefore, has nothing to do with her being unlovable. Dallas in *Stagecoach* is a prostitute, but Ringo falls in love with her regardless. Unlike Chihuahua, Dallas' love for Ringo does not interrupt the relationship of a married/engaged couple. This point is quite pivotal, as in Ford's attitudes toward romance, loving a woman is possible and fruitful if she is not the cause of a moral and traditional family/romantic union breaking down. Ford never suggests that Dallas has threatened a family in her capacity as a prostitute; even her exile from the town does not provide the audience with any reason to believe she has done so. Chihuahua is mainly associated with sexual deviations, whereas Dallas is primarily associated with tradi-

Part One—Fundamental Functions of Death Within the Narrative

tional motherhood. Thus, from the classic Western genre's point of view, Chihuahua does not have a chance for redemption and surviving the threat of death.

The next point is that Clementine represents virginity and professional virtue (in her capacity as a nurse, Clementine helps the wounded Chihuahua), so, morally speaking, she is the favorite of classic Hollywood films. Ford shows Clementine's devotion and fidelity to her fiancé in two ways. First, she has traveled a long way, from the East Coast of the United States, to join Holliday. The journey that she has undertaken to reach him indicates her love and care. Second, at the end of the film, after Holliday is killed during the OK Corral shootout, she stays in the town and becomes a schoolteacher. Clementine makes Tombstone her new home, and by adopting the teacher role, she fulfills the caring aspect of motherhood. She also shows signs of being aware of Wyatt's love for her, for she lets him kiss her on the cheek at the end of the film and permits him to call her by her first name. There is no amorous conversation between the two, but the viewers (and Clementine) can surmise that Wyatt will come back for her. So, the film ends suggestively, indicating that a potential cycle of life will form out of the combined moralities of east and west.

Kitses (2004, p. 61) writes, "Peter Wollen suggested that Earp's progress was an 'uncomplicated passage from nature to culture,' that his trajectory was from vengeful nomad to settled, married citizen. Rebutting Wollen, Bill Nichols accused the film of indulging a morbid delaying tactic in its narrative digressions from the revenge motif." Nichols' idea is valid regarding the usage of *Hamlet* in the film and the idea of delaying vengeance. I also argue that Wyatt's comfort with his emotions means that, unlike Hamlet, he does not choose a personal tragedy as a moral rod with which to punish people. Wood's and Gallaher's writings about Henry Fonda's persona relate to my argument. Wood (1980, p. 375) writes, "The values embodied in Fonda's persona—primarily a forward-looking idealism rooted in a belief in the development of civilization-are central to the Fordian ideology." Moreover, Gallagher (1986, p. 225) suggests that "Earp (like most Henry Fonda roles for Ford) is a hero pure who knows his mind, talks seldom, lopes calmly, gazes steadily, gets the job done." Because of the previously mentioned attitude of classic Hollywood cinema toward the death of leading heroes and the star personality that the character of Wyatt embodies, he kills the villains not for the sake of personal satisfaction but for the sake of banishing the serpents/Clantons from the upcoming garden that is civilized Tombstone.

2. The Cycle of Life

The conclusion of *My Darling Clementine* creates a coda to James Earp's death. Initially, James is the one who has an attitude favorable to the cycle of life: he is in love and wants to get married. By falling in love with Clementine, Wyatt's character comes closer to that of his deceased younger brother. Therefore, his romantic status at the end of the film creates moral symmetry with James' position at the beginning of the film. Consequently, the conclusion of the film suggests to the audience that the process of forging the cycle of life, previously interrupted by James' death, will perhaps proceed soon.

The lack of redemptive and moral romance results in a unique distinction between death and rebirth. We do not witness this distinction in Ford's films, but it is present in Kurosawa's films. The reason for this distinction is due to cultural differences. Eiko Ikegami, in her book *The Taming of the Samurai* (1995, p. 107), writes:

> [T]he philosophy of *Tendai-hongaku* (Philosophy of True Awareness), sometimes considered the medieval Buddhist intellectual paradigm, cultivated an ontological understanding of life and death, as represented by its conception of *shoji funi* (oneness of death and life) ... teachers of Pure Land sects of Buddhism characteristically preached death as a way to salvation—that is, as an opportunity for "rebirth in the pure land" (*o-jo*). Thus, the Pure Land devotee was taught to regard death as an opportunity to new existence rather than a fearsome enemy. The Zen sects are famous for their versions of the doctrine of the oneness of death and life. Furthermore, unlike native Shinto, Japanese Buddhism generally did not consider death itself a source of impurity (*kegare*).

I suggest two views on the connection between the theme of death and the cycle of life in its Japanese context based on Ikegami's writings: Buddhist (the oneness of death and life) and Shinto (death as the source of impurity). I propose that, in the case of Kurosawa's opus (including *Rashomon*), we witness a Buddhist treatment of death. The clearest example of this treatment in *Rashomon* is the third account of the samurai's murder, which is delivered by the spirit of the fallen samurai through the aid of a medium. The spirit is in hell because of the injustice that the samurai's wife and the bandit have inflicted on him. This depiction of the samurai's spirit suggests a union and close similarity between the cult of death and the cycle of life that are not entirely visible in Ford and Leone's films. Although in *Rashomon* the samurai has been killed, his spirit still enters the realm of the living. The spirit reports on the samurai's position in the afterlife, keeping his memory alive.

Furthermore, *Rashomon* portrays Kurosawa's attitude toward the

Part One—Fundamental Functions of Death Within the Narrative

morality of the deceased differently than classic Westerns. The warrior betrays his samurai code and follows his greed. However, he is not the villain. The film engages with various strategies to depict this heterogeneous status. In the first account of the murder, the samurai fights for his wife's honor; his fight begins in a moral sense before it turns physical—that is, when he is bound, and his wife is about to be raped, he struggles to free himself to go to her aid but fails to do so. In the second account, by contrast, Kurosawa portrays the samurai as unresponsive to his wife's pleas, which is not a crime, but rather an emotionally charged response to a traumatizing experience. In the third account, the samurai becomes a devastated romantic who kills himself. In the woodcutter's statement, he wants to live; this does not make the samurai evil, either, but it means that he lacks the moral convictions that his samurai codes and ethics require him to possess. This desire for life, which is natural and human, goes against the samurai codes that ask him to be ready to face the threat of death at any time. He ignores his class and moral codes. Thus his death is punishment, similar to Doc Holliday's death in *My Darling Clementine*, for both men have failed to live by the generic codes with which their respective films are concerned.

The next idea that merits scrutiny is that in *Rashomon*, the initial presence of a newborn baby carries a different ideological implication than its Fordian counterpart. In some of his films, Ford positions the infant in perilous situations, in much the same way that he does for his adult characters. The violence of the Apache Indians in *Stagecoach* threatens the life of Mrs. Mallory's newborn baby as much as the rest of the passengers. In another example, the newborn in *3 Godfathers* suffers from thirst and the harsh environment of the desert in a way analogous to that of his three guardians. Nevertheless, despite all these hardships, the infants of Ford's films are not abandoned; there are either a parent (as in *7 Women*) or kind strangers (as in *3 Godfathers*) present. This relationship is also reciprocal: the child alters the position of his/her guardians in the film, even if that guardian happens to be on the wrong side of the law. In *Rashomon*, the woodcutter adopts the abandoned baby. As the priest and woodcutter suggest, the toddler's parents may have had good reasons for leaving the child in the ruins of the temple.

In addition, Buddhist religion and philosophy, which influenced Kurosawa's vision significantly, provide insight on the relation between the rebirth of new attitudes and that of an individual. Related to this influence, I consider the writings of Campbell (2007, pp. 23–24): "In the Orient, we hear … of the 'cycle of birth or becoming' … and the call to the individual

2. The Cycle of Life

is to save ... himself: to purge away the wicked portion of his nature and to cultivate the godly." Furthermore, Nam-Lin Hur (2007, p. 17) focuses on the notion of rebirth and its connection to an individual's death: "Within the system of karmic causality, as LaFleur puts it: Death will result in rebirth, and rebirth always poses the possibility of either progress or slippage to another location in the taxonomy."

The parallel between Kurosawa and Ford can be found in this notion that the child can alter the adoptive parent's position in the story, and perhaps give a new direction to their lives. In this regard, Kurosawa and Ford imbue children with similar ideological implications. The child's position in *Rashomon*, similar to children in Ford's films, indicates the hope for a better future. Robin Wood, in his short review of *Rashomon*,[1] has the following to say regarding the presence of the baby and the ending in *Rashomon*: "His [woodcutter] adopting the baby (although he and his family are near starvation-level) follows logically from the scathing denunciation of self-serving egoism that is the central impulse of his version of the story: rising above the moral squalor of his time and the physical squalor of his environment, he performs the action that at once establishes his heroic status and redeems the film's almost desperate, almost nihilist view of humanity."

In Ford's films, once the hero fully has merged with his generic obligations, the innocent people survive the threat of death. In Kurosawa's films, the hero's new position means that he is an involved member of the human society. This is his way of showing the impact of wrongdoings on the community and the hero's attempt to respond to this problem. This moment of involvement is when the narrative usually ends; it marks the new status of the hero in the story. This involvement does not mean a physical or an emotional integration with society, similar to some of Ford's characters (e.g., Ethan in *The Searchers*). Rather, such involvement means recognizing the presence of better choices in life that society has to offer. In the case of Kurosawa, I refer to the ending of *Sanjuro*, when the hero realizes that his way of life has not been wise, for he has killed many people unnecessarily. This realization makes him a more sensible and prudent warrior.

Most of Leone's heroes, similar to those of Kurosawa, are not involved in sexual/romantic relationships. This attitude of the hero positions him at the margins of the cycle of life. The script of *A Fistful of Dollars* clarifies the hero's emotional loneliness through a single line: "I don't find home that great." However, there is no backstory that explains why the hero dislikes home.

Part One—Fundamental Functions of Death Within the Narrative

This being said, the hero in this film, by killing one family and saving another, contributes to the preservation of the cycle of life. Thus, his position on the idea of family life is clear: he kills those who disrupt its primitive functions. Kitses (2004, p. 257) suggests, "As in Ford, the family is a central value in Leone, but it is a value lost, corrupted or destroyed, a structuring absence." I would challenge Kitses' comments by suggesting that there is a similarity between Ford's and Leone's attitudes toward criminal families. The films of both directors assign the hero the task of exterminating problematic families (for example, the Rojo clan, the Clanton family or the Plummer boys). Therefore, the only aspect of Wexman's idea of dynastic nostalgia that works in the case of Leone's films is the death of all villains. The substitution of a conventional and idealized happy ending with an ultraviolent one not only indicates a skeptical perspective on Western genre conventions but also emphasizes the point that the hero, generically and ideologically, does not settle into this civilization and its ethics.

The hero is not part of a potential cycle of life due to the function of community in Leone's representation of the west. Kitses (2004, p. 256) writes on this matter, "In Leone, the wilderness and its brutishness have invaded the community itself. The thrust is to see all in savage dress; a West defined without progress. Death rules: the logic of the action and imagery of the films is to see the frontier as a vast cemetery." Civilization has no privileged position in Leone's *Dollar* trilogy. In Leone's version of the west, towns are usually far more dangerous than the wilderness. In *A Fistful of Dollars*, most of the killings happen inside San Miguel. This scenario is a departure from Ford's films, where the wilderness is typically the wasteland, the location where the tragedy begins. For example, in *The Searchers*, Ethan's family (who are massacred by Indians) reside on a farm far from any town. Likewise, in *Fort Apache*, two American soldiers are murdered by Indians in the desert, away from any civilized community.

The leading villain in Leone's films, similar to Ford's villains, engages with one of the two following strategies to break the cycle of life (although it is worth pointing out that this choice of strategy is not a conscious act on the part of the villain—rather, it is due to his corrupt nature). One strategy is what I call "permanent invalidity," and the second is "temporary invalidity."

Permanent invalidity means that the death of a mother and/or her child/children breaks their family's cycle of life for good. This kind of invalidity usually occurs in cases when a woman is married to a criminal or a man is married to a morally compromised woman. This strategy does not

2. The Cycle of Life

give the hero the goal of defending the family. For example, in *A Fistful of Dollars*, because Consuelo Baxter is married to the criminal/corrupt sheriff of the town, she does not deserve to survive the threat of death. Early in the film, Leone provides her with what I see as a "morality test"; she has the chance to show her sense of morality when the hero brings Marisol to her household. Consuelo could mend Marisol's broken cycle of life by returning the captured woman to her family. However, she exchanges Marisol for her captured son; Consuelo lacks the courage to sacrifice her corrupt cycle of life for the sake of others. Later, at the end of the massacre in which Consuelo's husband and son are murdered, her position is changed from a strong mother and wife to a weak widow, from the keeper of a cycle of life to the mourner of a dead one when she sees her son's corpse.

Temporary invalidity, by contrast, means that the villain interrupts the function of the cycle of life, separating a mother from her family. This separation means that the villain, even if only for a brief time, takes away the source of nurture from the child/children. Consequently, the mother can no longer perform her nurturing abilities. The way Leone establishes Marisol's initial position links to this point, as he shows her behind the iron bars of her prison-house. The henchmen of the Rojo clan prevent Marisol's young son from visiting his mother. I contend that her dire situation can mean the imprisonment of motherhood and the traditional moralities that Marisol's marriage and previously settled life represent. As mentioned previously, in Ford's works those individuals who are involved in sexual relationships that do not amount to a traditional marriage will be killed during the film. However, there is an exception to this rule: if a female character is forced into this kind of relationship, she survives the threat of death and reunites with her family (e.g., Debbie in *The Searchers*). This exception is also part of Leone's text. In this scenario, he provides the hero with the goal of reuniting mother and child. In fulfilling this purpose, the hero redeems himself from his past actions toward Marisol. To be able to keep her family safe, Marisol subsequently leaves town.

Leone portrays civilization (or at least the town) as the wasteland that is the locus of death, tragedy, and moral destruction. Even destruction of villain does not transform this wasteland completely.

3

The Cult of Death

The *cult of death* is a common concept among various cultures. The roots of this cultural phenomenon in western culture, as Erasmo (2012) argues, trace back to primitive civilizations that resided in Europe. In classic Hollywood films, this cult is a significant aspect of the plot. Hagin (2010, pp. 66–67) writes on this matter:

> I will adopt the term "cult" to refer to this group that retains the memory of the deceased that makes sure that the dead do not simply retreat into an anonymous mass. We might also, following an analysis by Jean-François Lyotard, compare this with a certain function of the Athenian "beautiful death," in which the dead escape their death and are perpetuated through a collective name (patronym, eponym, nationality). According to Lyotard, the collective name assures within itself the perenniality of individual proper names. A cult, or a collectivity, is needed ... for the dead to be retained, to escape their death.

According to the above notion, the raison d'être of the cult of death is accepting the physical death of an individual. However, the cult of death also celebrates the memory of the deceased, which results in the preservation of memories of the dead. I further argue that this preservation keeps aspects of the deceased's personality alive for the cult members. During an individual's lifetime, their actions and patterns of behavior contribute to a consciousness or personality that is unique to them. This may, in turn, rub off or otherwise leave an impression on the people with whom they interact. If others remember the unique characteristics of the individual, they may pass them on in a variety of ways, such as verbally or through written texts, paintings or films. Thus, in some respects, an individual's consciousness and memories continue to subsist even after his death as his friends/family remember his actions. Related to this idea, Norbert Elias (1985, p. 67) writes, "Death hides no secret.... What survives is what he or she [the departed] has given to other people, what stays in their memory."

This chapter furthers the ideas of Hagin by arguing that (a) the cult of death provides its members with an opportunity to remember the deeds

3. The Cult of Death

and actions of the deceased; (b) an individual death, beyond its tragic quality, can function as motivation for the cult members (mainly the hero) to take moral actions (or even villainous actions in the case of an antagonist); (c) the cult of death can bring people together to mirror the outcomes of a shared ordeal, although the reader should remember that the responses and reactions to this "shared ordeal" can differ due to different personalities and cultural backgrounds; and (d) the actions and achievements of the cult members function as part of a schematic plan that assists the audience in making sense of the film's story.

I have identified two attitudes for the cult of death. One is what I call the "historical cult"—that is, the preserved memory of the deceased based on reality. The historical cult preserves the memory of an individual's life without any falsification. Therefore, in the plot, the cult of death remembers the deceased (e.g., James Earp in *My Darling Clementine*) for who he was, rather than as a larger-than-life legendary figure. This kind of cult usually has two motivations: (a) vengeance and (b) bringing civil order to a community.

The second type of cult of death is the "mythical cult." This version ignores some aspects of the deceased's life in order to create a myth out of his somewhat dubious actions. In other words, the "mythical cult" eschews the shortcomings of the deceased and portrays him as a flawless, idealistic figure. Consequently, in this type of cult, the morality of the dead character motivates the remaining moral characters to contribute to the progress of society (e.g., Colonel Thursday in *Fort Apache*).

There is one exception in the case of *Rashomon* concerning the cult of death. In this film, there is no collective or shared memory of the dead person, which leads to each cult member uniquely remembering the deceased. This fragmented attitude toward death does not have the same straightforward ideological quality for the community as the other two cults of death. Through this scenario, the film criticizes the very essence of truth. The questions here, in contrast to historical and or mythical cults, are not "who did what?" and "what was the effect of the deceased's actions on community/society?" but rather "how did the deceased die?" and "to what extent is he responsible for his destruction and the destruction of those close to him?"

In Ford's *My Darling Clementine*, James Earp (Don Garner), the youngest of the Earp brothers (he is only 18 years old), is killed by the Clanton family early in the film. Hagin calls this type of demise "initial death." In Hagin's (2010, p. 5) words, "Initial ... deaths can be meaningful *in relation*

Part One—Fundamental Functions of Death Within the Narrative

to the future, by being causes of subsequent events." Due to this loss, Wyatt Earp will come out of retirement as a marshal and ultimately face the Clanton boys. Likewise, Kitses (2004, p. 57) argues that James' death "represents a murder of the civilized spirit and the feminine, a martyrdom and unspeakable tragedy signaled by the three brothers standing motionless around the body in the dark downpour." There are two points here: First, Kitses talks about the remaining Earp brothers gathering around James. Ford utilizes the same style as *Stagecoach*, in which a group of men assemble and the camera (as it does in *My Darling Clementine*) portrays them in a medium shot from behind. The parallel in the two films is about togetherness. In the earlier film the stagecoach passengers come together to celebrate the new life; in *My Darling Clementine*, the remaining Earp brothers come together to mourn the lost life of their younger brother. Their togetherness results in the formation of a cult of death.

In Ford's films, the family-formed cult is what I describe as a "historical cult of death"—that is, a cult that recognizes the shortcomings of the dead individual as well as his achievements. The part of Kitses' argument that relates to James' historical cult of death is his character's portrayal as feminine in the light of traditional views on gender. James is portrayed as feminine, for, as Virgil Earp says, "he can cook as good as Mom." Also, in contrast to his brothers, he has no facial hair, which suggests that he is not physically a grown man yet. I argue that since the Earps' mother is physically absent from the film, James' cooking abilities (which are a nurturing aspect of mothers in a traditionalist view) represent her. Furthermore, Wood (1996, p. 175) points out that "women for Ford are at once the pretext for civilization ... and ... the guarantee of its continuity. And he characteristically endows his women with the finest attributes: strength, fortitude, integrity, nobility. The price of this is of course that their role remains at bottom firmly 'traditional,' whatever apparent deviations the film produces." Related to *My Darling Clementine*, this arrangement can mean that although James' death is the initial death of the film, it also signifies the destruction of a potential family/cycle of life. His death likewise serves as a motivation for his brothers to change their immediate goal (taking their cattle to California) and stay in town to find their brother's murderers.

James Earp's grave in Tombstone is a monument reminding viewers of a corrupt and uncivilized episode in the history of Tombstone. Ken Warpole (in Erasmo, 2012, p. 63) writes, "The place of burial and tomb, as a representation of the deceased, has a transformative effect on the landscape or burial setting that becomes associated with death and the identities of

3. The Cult of Death

those buried there." This transformation of the place of death occurs in *My Darling Clementine* when Wyatt gives his monologue on James' grave. He recognizes the uncivilized atmosphere of Tombstone (the town's name explicitly evokes the threat of death). His new goal is making society a better and safer place for young people like James. Ford, in showing spectators James' grave and referring to it verbally later in the film, emphasizes how significant James' death has been in influencing the film's ideology. Here we should remind ourselves of Hagin's doctrine that the initial death is meaningful for the future, as well as the importance of the burial as a sign for this future. It should also be mentioned that sequences of funerals and graveyards occur in the context of other forms of death in the Western films (and not only in that of the initial death).

The cult of death can bring people together, reminding them of their duty to their fellow men. The proof of this point in *My Darling Clementine* is when Billy Clanton (John Ireland) kills Doc Holliday's mistress, Chihuahua, and Holliday subsequently joins the remaining Earp brothers to fight against the Clanton family. Holliday's response to the actions of the villains who committed murder is similar to that of Earp brothers. The result of this response is that the characters achieve their goal of revenge and destroy the antagonistic force. Thus, beyond being a motif of the plot, vengeance creates a sense of morality as well. Therefore, in most of the classic fiction films, the hero accepts the death of his loved ones quickly, and the action goes on. As Hagin (2010, p. 45) notes, "Generally, for death to be meaningful in relation to the future in a classical Hollywood film, the event should not overwhelm the remaining individuals in the world of the film to the point of paralysis. It is not that the death needs to be undone and ignored—it does influence the causal storyline—but it also cannot be fatal to it. The film does not stop to mourn and work through the loss for several months or years." The narrative must continue to assure the viewers that the dead people's memories will be propagated.

This argument is illustrative with regard to the intertextual position of *Hamlet* in *My Darling Clementine*. The theme of revenge is a prominent aspect of both texts. Furthermore, Ford is concerned not only with the motif of vengeance in *Hamlet* but also with the idea of death that the following extracted verses from the play (3.1.57–68) suggest: "To be, or not to be, that is the question ... To die, to sleep, No more; and by a sleep to say we end.... To die, to sleep; [to] sleep, perchance to dream—ay, there's the rub: For in that sleep of death what dreams may come, when we have shuffled off this mortal coil ... the dread of something after death."

Part One—Fundamental Functions of Death Within the Narrative

The usage of Shakespeare's soliloquy contextualizes the reaction of the film's characters to the idea of death. For example, Doc Holliday, who suffers from tuberculosis, recites the above verses. There are two reasons for Holliday's reaction to his potential death: first, Hollywood films are more concerned with tangible action than the kind of psychological reflection to which the Elizabethan/Jacobean soliloquy gives voice; and second, it could be the secular nature of Westerns in general, and Ford's films in particular. Wood (1980, p. 375) writes on this matter, "The function of religion in Ford is essentially social rather than metaphysical." In Ford's films, religion and its myriad concepts function more like the social glue that keeps people together (as a performance of *Hamlet* would bring the community together) rather than as a celestial doctrine that transparently affects people's lives. I would add that this secularism is a natural aspect of the evolution of mysticism and religion and their position in society. As Campbell (2008, p. 213) points out, "When a civilization has passed from a mythological to a secular point of view, the older images are no longer felt." In most classic Westerns (such as a John Ford or Howard Hawks films), death is not a source of fear or horror for the protagonist or those who follow and support the rules and norms of society. The death of a friend or loved one motivates the hero and his friends, family or fellow citizens to question their responsibility toward the memory of the dead. As a result, decent citizens come together. This togetherness forms the cult of death.

I note that every now and then the audience may encounter a situation where the threat of death intimidates the good (i.e., law-abiding) people of society. The epitome of this situation is found in *High Noon* (dir. Fred Zinnemann), which, by the standards of its time, was not a conventional Western in the same spirit of Ford, Hawks, and Anthony Mann films. Instead of leaving town with his young bride, Will Kane (Gary Cooper) decides to stay and face the man who wants to kill him. None of the town's inhabitants want to help their once beloved marshal keep law and order in town. On a peripheral level, the plot is conventional: a marshal must face a criminal gang in order to save his prominent position within the classic Western genre's conventions and, in effect, to protect law and order. However, the core message of the film is quite unconventional because the town's inhabitants ignore their social and moral duty toward their marshal.

The next related argument to the cult of death is that, as a part of the Western film tradition and many classic genres, the villain's death usually means the death of his memories as well. A clear example is the case of Papa Clanton's death. At the end of the OK Corral shootout, Wyatt can kill

3. The Cult of Death

him but refuses to do so. Thus, as Wyatt says, the old man Clanton "can always remember his murdered sons" and suffer. The villain-father is not able to commemorate his sons' deaths within the community's hemisphere, so he must leave. As Wyatt puts it, "Get out of the town; start wandering." However, the old man tries to shoot Wyatt (after all, the former is the villain), but Morgan Earp kills him. (It is rather significant that Morgan shoots the old Clanton, for he is the oldest of the Earp brothers and has seniority over the Earp cult.) Papa Clanton's death means that no one in the Clanton family remains alive to establish a cult.

To understand how a historical cult of death can contribute to the future of community within a classic American Western, I will focus on the central hero of *My Darling Clementine*. McBride's (2003, p. 341) report on the historical background of the Earp brothers is of interest here: "The actual Earp brothers considered themselves primarily 'sporting men' rather than lawmen and were known to their enemies as 'the fighting pimps.' In Tombstone, they served as the hired guns of the Republican business community in opposition to the ranchers, mostly Democrats, who protected outlaws such as the Clantons." In his movie, Ford recontextualizes the historical Wyatt Earp. Allen Barra (in Cohen, 2003, p. 204) writes, "Historians even now judge him [Wyatt Earp] not by his own achievements or by the standards of lawmen in his own time and place but by the absurdly unrealistic ideals of the saintly Hollywood characters." Barra criticizes the lack of a rigorous historical approach toward Wyatt Earp. In the myth created by Hollywood, Wyatt is an idealistic hero rather than a historical reality. Films about the Earp brothers portray Wyatt more as a secular saint than as a conservative marshal. Additionally, these films are more concerned with Wyatt's moral achievements, as opposed to how he engages with the law of the time. In Ford's approach to the myth of Wyatt Earp, the hero is motivated by justice as well as revenge, for he aims to bring law and order back to Tombstone. Wyatt approaches his brother's murder as a legitimate reason for cleansing the entire community of Tombstone of the unethical deeds of the Clantons.

My Darling Clementine is the cinematic setting where perhaps the most famous Wyatt Earp known to popular culture is born. Cohen (2003, p. 207) sums up Henry Fonda's interpretation of Wyatt Earp as follows: "Ford's Wyatt (Henry Fonda) is thoughtful, soft-spoken, and decisive. He exhibits a deferential sense of authority; he would rather talk than use a gun but is a faster and more accurate shot than anyone, including Doc Holliday. He may fudge the line between personal revenge and law, but he shows no hint of self-doubt or lack of conviction." The question is: What does Wyatt do

Part One—Fundamental Functions of Death Within the Narrative

for the film's ideology toward history? As Kitses (2004, p. 57) writes, "Structurally and dramatically, the film [*My Darling Clementine*] proposes that the violent elimination of anarchy is the final act in a historical process that initially involves the establishment and defense of law, culture, and religion." I would add the following to Kitses' argument: Encountering the Clanton family results in establishing order in society, which ensures the survival of individual freedom and religion, the two ideological lexicons that contributed immensely to forming the American identity. The church scene emphasizes the latter aspect. During this portion of the film, the entire community is in a newly built church in Tombstone. The absent people are Doc Holliday, his mistress (the two have sexual relations out of wedlock, and so their morality is compromised) and the Clanton family (who are the criminals). Through Wyatt and Clementine's dance in this scene, Ford portrays a union between the symbol of western law (Wyatt) and the symbol of eastern civilization (Clementine). This union, in its symbolic function, illustrates the legitimacy of the cult of death in the film. When law-abiding and decent citizens come together in this way, the cult of death has moral foundations, whereas a cult forged by the antagonists (to be precise, villains in other films as well as in *My Darling Clementine*) does not have that moral authority. This moral legitimacy is beneficial for Clementine as well. At the end of the film, she stays in Tombstone. Her former sweetheart/fiancé is dead, and she intends to work as a schoolteacher. By providing the children with an education, she contributes to building a future for the society, much like Wyatt, who, in his role as the marshal, served the same purpose. Therefore, Ford's Earp is not only an officer of the law who faced a handful of thugs in the 19th century; he also functions as a symbol representing American ideals of the 20th century.

If we want to understand the position of the cult of death in Kurosawa's films, we need to understand the position of the deceased in Japanese society. In the context of Japanese culture, the spirits of the dead still influence the lives of those left behind in the realm of the living. Stephen Turnbull, in his book *The Samurai and the Sacred* (2006, p. 176), writes, "Japanese ancestor worship, which is not a separate religious sect but a series of beliefs integrated into the overall religious system, ensures that death does not extinguish a person's involvement in the life of his family. Instead of a complex series of rituals designed to keep the ancestors peaceful and content in the successive stages through which they will pass, this continuity is assured." This cultural attitude is similar to the idea of the cult of death in western thought, suggesting that it exists in Japanese culture as well.

3. The Cult of Death

In the samurai culture, the cult of death has one more function: it presents the ideas and mentalities of the warrior class toward death, rather than only the deceased's friends' and family's reaction to his death. Ikegami (1995, p. 281) points out that "Tsunetomo ... believes '[death] was the gateway to proper induction as a samurai in the first place. Only through learning how to die honorably could a man attain the mindset of a true samurai, in peacetime as well as during war.' Furthermore, one could live as a true samurai only by cultivating a state of mind that dispensed with rational calculation, a mentality that Tsunetomo called *shini gurui* or 'death frenzy.'" There are several points to explore in the notion of "death frenzy." Although it is not part of the samurai tradition in *bushido*, this concept is relevant for studying the cult of death in the case of Kurosawa's samurai films. His characters are similar to the characters of Ford's and Leone's films in that, when faced with a life-threatening situation, they usually respond calmly to such a threat. Samurai ethics and the typical characteristics of the *jidaigeki*'s tragic hero also contribute to this calm response. I have explained the idea of the Japanese tragic hero in the introduction to this book: Thornton (2008, p. 52) writes that the tragic hero "loses all there is to lose in life and dies in great resentment and suffering. The tragic hero is portrayed as conventionally noble and done in by the villains, traitors, or fate." A tragic hero faces danger (including the threat of death) with a calm disposition. Likewise, a true samurai is one who learns through training and instruction about the ethics and traditions of his class to die with honor. Ikegami (1995, p. 23) explains the concept of honor as follows: "The notion of honor not only is expressed as a concern for one's social evaluation but is profoundly connected with one's dignity, self-esteem, and identity. One's honor is the image of oneself in the social mirror, and that image affects one's self-esteem and one's behavior." Based on Ikegami's writings, I argue that a samurai's honor is also a social necessity. These social expectations are one significant difference between the attitudes of samurai and those of Western films regarding death. In the latter category, unless the hero possesses legal authority (e.g., sheriff/marshal or cavalry officer), society initially is not concerned with a lone gunman's sense of honor or his safety.

Kurosawa's films, in tandem with most of Ford's Westerns, favor a historical cult of death. However, in *Rashomon*, the audience witnesses a unique case regarding the cult of death—it is neither historical nor mythical. One of the primary functions of the cult of death in epic/action films is that it contributes to the clarity of the film's conclusion. However, Kurosawa's *Rashomon* takes an unusual approach to the cult, which occurs once

Part One—Fundamental Functions of Death Within the Narrative

in his films and is absent from the films of Ford and Leone. It creates a somewhat ambiguous ending for the film.

The fragmentation of the cult of death happens due to the nature of *Rashomon*'s narrative, as it tells the same story from different viewpoints. The fragmentation of the cult is rooted in the duplicity of the characters—not only do they see events differently, but they also lie about their observations. Different characters have contradictory views and approaches toward the deceased and his memory; they do not have the moral authority to keep the memory of the dead samurai alive. A fragmented cult of death does not produce a unified attitude toward the deceased and his actions. Likewise, this film's conclusion does not provide absolute truth about the samurai's mysterious death. As Goodwin (1994, p. 27) points out, in Kurosawa's films, "truth is not to be found within a single character but rather among characters engaged in dynamic, mutable conflict."

The woodcutter's position in this film is thought-provoking since he does not mention to the court that he saw who killed the samurai and that the other witnesses' testimonies are false. Richie (1996, p. 72) argues that "we are given very little [information] for disbelieving what is said by any of the original three because their stories, if lies are not the kind of lies which one tells of escaping punishment, and this would seem to be the usual reason for lying.... Each pleads guilty." I agree with Richie's point and suggest that these lies do not serve the purpose of catharsis. The characters do not appear to confess to crime out of shame or remorse. Kurosawa does not provide his audience with any clear visual or verbal indications to think otherwise.

Each of the testimonies is, in fact, an account of the murder that draws antithetical schemas for dividing the attitudes toward the cult of death. The audience cannot agree on one specific version of the story. In the first account of the murder, Tajōmaru—the bandit—admits to killing the samurai. He also says that the samurai's wife convinced him that since she had been raped in front of her husband, she "cannot go on living, knowing her shame is known to two men." One man must die, and she must become the wife/mistress of the murderer. This promise of a potential sexual triumph stands in stark contrast to Ford's films, where this promise is made only to law-abiding citizens or characters redeemed from their past moral failings; in this way, the sexual promise only benefits those who want to settle down and create a family. As said by Wood, the sexual relationship between a man and a woman in Ford's films has no value per se; rather, family is a value. In Leone's work, as Kitses argues, the lack of this value has affected society gravely.

3. The Cult of Death

Based on the Japanese social codes of the medieval era in which *Rashomon* takes place, the woman is the symbol of homemaking and motherhood (although the western society also overwhelmed women with similar codes during the medieval period). Wakita Haruko (2006, p. 13), in *Women in Medieval Japan: Motherhood, Household Management and Sexuality*, writes, "while the wife [in medieval] Japan had overall responsibility for managing the household, her most fundamental duties were motherhood, ensuring the succession of the *ie* [family system] and sexual love, which is the source of motherhood and a symbol of prosperity." In *Rashomon*, the bandit's chance to be involved with the samurai's wife does not mean that Kurosawa celebrates and advocates societal deprivation. Similar to the unredeemable criminals of Ford and Leone's films, his character is killed off from the story.

In the bandit's account, he portrays the samurai as a man of honor. Tajōmaru, as described in the court scene, is a famous and notorious criminal. This fearsome reputation notwithstanding, Kurosawa portrays the samurai as the most competent adversary Tajōmaru had ever fought. There are two reasons for this: first, Tajōmaru embellishes his swordsmanship, and second, the samurai was zealous in his attempt to defeat the bandit and restore his wife's honor. Considering that he had failed to defend his wife from rape, the samurai seeks to restore honor through violence.

These notions of honorific violence in *Rashomon* and the cult of death in its samurai sense are opposed to each other in the second and third accounts of the murder. In the former account, provided by the samurai's wife, the samurai's death does not carry any ideological meaning: it is a cold-hearted murder. She argues that the death of her husband is a product of her rape and loss of face in front of him.

Her claim of killing the samurai appears to be possible from a psychological perspective. She is ashamed of what has happened to her, and since she is powerless in front of the bandit, she attacks her husband. She protests that her husband, after the rape, was cold to her: "he said nothing, he did nothing." This can mean that she was looking for any form of affection and sympathy that the samurai could have shown her after the rape incident. The dishonored woman goes as far as begging her husband to kill her, but to no avail. The samurai's silence in the face of his wife's begging and screaming, on first viewing, may suggest shock. He is composed and cold, but this does not necessarily mean that viewing his wife's rape has not traumatized him. In *Bushido* (2001, p. 11), Nitobe writes that Buddhism "furnished a sense of calm trust in fate, a quiet submission to the inevitable, that stoic composure in sight of danger or calamity, that disdain of life and friendliness with death." Based on this notion, the second account of the murder illustrates the samurai (after witnessing the tragedy) as a character who follows a Buddhist approach after he witnesses his wife's rape. By contrast, his cold behavior may also suggest contempt for his wife. However, I disagree with this reading; Wakita (2006, p. 17) notes that "[t]he *ie* was ruled by the male head, to whom the wife was subordinate, and there is no doubt that the wife was a chattel of her husband." It appears that in witnessing the shame of his wife/property in a medieval sense, the samurai holds her responsible for the rape, which explains his lack of emotion in response to his wife's pleas to kill her.

The samurai's spirit projects the third account of the murder and thus the third annex of the cult of death. A medium conveys this statement in court. The samurai's soul, according to the medium, is in darkness and suffering, for, as the spirit says, his wife after the rape asked the bandit to kill her husband. Once the samurai was untied by the bandit (after his wife had fled), he killed himself out of despair, not for honor. The possibility of the samurai's suicide means that his wife would be free from her husband's depressing and shameful looks. Her position in the film changes from that of a mere victim to a murderer.

The final account of the murder belongs to the woodcutter. In his statement, the samurai at first refuses to fight to reclaim his wife, because she has told the bandit that if he wants to marry her, he must fight her husband. Nitobe (2001, pp. 29–30) writes that among the warrior class, "death for a cause unworthy of dying for, was called a 'dog's death.'" I argue that the samurai's refusal to fight saves him from the "dog's death." The warrior sees his wife as someone who is not worth fighting for, and so he says, "I do not want to risk my life for such a woman." Kurosawa thus shows the samurai's change of position from a warrior to a dishonored person.

Hitherto, I have written on the importance of family as a dominant force in forming the cult of death in the films of Ford and Kurosawa. The absence of family and its values in Leone's works creates unique characteristics and functions for the cult of death, distinguishing Leone's approach to the cult from Ford's and Kurosawa's interpretations of the same concept.

To begin with, in Leone's films, once the hero survives the threat of death and the villain is dead, there will be no cult of death in the narrative. For example, in the case of *The Good, the Bad and the Ugly*, Tuco and Blondie survive the threat of death, while Angel Eyes (who is, in fact, the villain of the film) is killed at the end. There is no family member/friend/

3. The Cult of Death

gang member to form his cult of death. I have previously argued that in Ford's films, the lack of a cult of death encodes the message that the film does not honor the deceased's life; ergo his morality and memories will not survive. Since the classic Western's attitude toward the dead does not have a significant position in Leone's Westerns, vengeance motivates the lone hero to face up to the villain (as is the case with *For a Few Dollars More*) rather than the memory of the deceased. In most of Leone's films, the members of the cult of death are never family members; they are merely friends. This means that the larger society/community does not contribute to the formation of the cult of death. In Leone's films, the criminal families and clans overwhelm the community and its values.

In *A Fistful of Dollars*, the portrayal of the hero as a lone gunman for hire who has no affiliation with any social/community groups is necessary to emphasize the depth of the corruption in society. Making a fortune is the hero's initial motivation. Leone does not define his film's hero in the context of traditional morality or a revenge story. As a result, the two main elements that would motivate the hero to be part of a potential cult are absent from this film.

The hero's position, however, is not as lonely as it appears, as he befriends Silvanito, the town's innkeeper. Kitses (2004, p. 256) sees "friendship" as a significant strategy of Leone's storytelling method: "The one saving value of Leone's dark West is friendship, the interrogated value—ambiguous, expedient, comically unstable—that runs through the films and brightens its principles." This friendship serves three functions in relation the theme of death. First, it has an informative function for the audience. Through conversation between these characters, we are constantly *au fait* with the hero's schemes. The hero uses death and dead people as strategies to manipulate the criminal families (i.e., he kills four of the Baxter men to attract the attention of the Rojo clan). Second, the hero's relationship with Silvanito provides him with a friend who, later in the film when he is badly injured, will help him to recover his health. Third, this friendship contributes to the destruction of the potential cult of death at the end of the film. In the film's conclusion, the Rojos have captured Silvanito, so the hero comes back to town and kills the entire Rojo household. The death of the villains in *A Fistful of Dollars* shows the similarity between the approaches of Ford, Kurosawa, and Leone. Their films deal violently with a criminal family or clan that can establish a cult of death. The leading hero, either alone or with the help of the supporting hero, destroys such a family or clan. Thus, in *A Fistful of Dollars* Ramon Rojo's death has two functions. First, it is an

Part One—Fundamental Functions of Death Within the Narrative

event that Hagin (2010, p. 5) calls the *story-terminating death*, "which ends a storyline and is an effect of previous events." Second, the death of the most likely person to initiate a cult of death means that there will be no cult of death for the Rojo clan.

Moreover, in his films, Leone's portrayal of the individuality of the leader of a villainous group is more detailed than Ford's and Kurosawa's portrayals of Indians or bandits. The individuality of the leader of these collectives (for example, the bandits of *Seven Samurai* or the Indians of *Stagecoach*) is usually not one of the main concerns for these two directors; instead, the entire group usually represents the depraved ethics. Even if there is a villainous individual (such as Scar in *The Searchers*), his presence on screen is not emphasized with the same visual and temporal weight of Leone's villains. Leone shows the intensity and violent nature of the villains repeatedly through extreme close-ups of their faces and guns. In his films, the primary villain is that dictatorial and charismatic individual who keeps the group together, whereas in Ford's and Kurosawa's films, the violent ideology or social savagery are the forces that hold a villainous group together.

The final point is that in *A Fistful of Dollars*, Leone shows the hero (and, indeed, the audience) two types of families. The crime families are the the Rojo brothers and the Baxters, respectively, and the traditional-moral family (which is temporarily torn apart through no fault of its own) consists of Marisol, her husband, and her son. So, in contrast to Ford's films, Leone does not give the audience any traditionally good and stable families. Although Marisol's family is traditional, they are powerless to defend their moral integrity. As discussed previously, the deaths of the Rojos and the Baxters mean the termination of any potential cult of death. Leone's films, similar to Ford's, provide reasons why the villains cannot form such a cult. The difference between the works of the Leone and those of Ford is that the former's films do not place much emphasis on traditional values such as education, romance and redemption, whereas Ford's films are all about these values. There is no Shakespeare recital or conventional and moral romance in Leone's west. Instead, the only source of redemption is involvement with others' misfortunes short of any romantic attachment. This places Leone's interpretation of romance and issues related to a character's redemption closer to that of Kurosawa.

Part Two

The Hero's Position and the Theme of Death in Battle

4
Death, Personal Conflict and Battle

Robert McKee suggests, due to traditions of storytelling that Aristotle outlined in his *Poetics* (335 BCE), that the hero of any story is supposed to endure various kinds of pressure. This endurance, as McKee (1999, p. 100) writes, depicts the true self of the hero: "True character is revealed in the choices a human being makes under pressure—the greater the pressure, the deeper the revelation, the truer the choice to the character's essential nature." One of the most prominent pressures that a character can face is the threat of death. The hero's encounter with such a threat in battle tests the limits of his emotional, moral, and physical strength as no other type of death can, since a battle between armies shows historical confrontations among different political and ideological attitudes.

I have identified three sets of conflicts in the films covered in this study that deal with the concept of battle. These conflicts include the "personal conflict," the "inner-group conflict" and the "external conflict." The relation between the theme of death and these conflicts clarifies the function of the battlefield in a film's story concerning the morality of the hero, as well as that of the group to which he belongs. In this chapter, I study the hero's personal conflict in the films of Ford, Kurosawa, and Leone. The following chapters will deal with the other two types of conflict.

Personal conflict refers to those emotional issues of the leading and supporting heroes that affect their actions. This inward struggle is one of the ancient traits of the hero. In literature and fiction films, the hero traditionally faces a variety of difficulties and ordeals. Personal conflicts, as part of that pressure, can reveal the hero's ethos regarding what he is rather than what he appears to be.

Ford's *Fort Apache*, both visually and through dialogue (thanks to Frank Nugent's script), contextualizes the leading hero's emotional issues and their relation to the theme of death. The film begins with the arrival of Colonel Owen Thursday (Henry Fonda), a former general in the Union Army, at Fort Apache, a military base on the western frontier. Thursday

4. Death, Personal Conflict and Battle

believes that he has been pushed away (he offers no further explanations) to the fort by army officials in Washington, D.C. As a result, he is frustrated with his new post. Moreover, he fails to adapt to his new life. His attitude is set against the veteran officers and soldiers of the fort, most notably Captain York (John Wayne). Consequently, many disagreements arise between Thursday and the fort's inhabitants. This film dwells on the hero's conflict through the constant dispute and debates on national policies (particularly the treatment of Apache Indians).

Thursday, by not adapting to his environment, unconsciously creates conflict with other officers in the fort. Ford portrays Thursday as a fallen hero in an alien geographical and political landscape. Darby (2006, p. 83) writes on this point, "Colonel Owen Thursday (Henry Fonda) represents a transient figure in the ... film, a man who is significantly measured by his many failures to accept frontier life." The strategies for this portrayal are plenty. The film's script suggests Thursday's negative and skeptical attitude toward his new professional and social circumstances through his first line of dialogue: "What a country; from mud hole to mud hole." His interruption of the dance in honor of George Washington's birthday also challenges the balance of the fort's harmony and social dynamics. Russell Campbell, as quoted in McBride (2003, p. 452), describes these Fordian dance sequences as "occasions for carefree spontaneity and the affectionate celebration of fellowship within strict traditional conventions." Thursday's interruption of the dance is indicative of how he challenges this celebration of the harmonious life of the fort. Therefore, his actions gradually put him on the margin of the social life in Fort Apache. Stripped of his former rank of general during the Civil War (Ford does not explain why this is the case) and now a colonel, Thursday yearns for recognition and revalidation. Ford also establishes Thursday's presence as an inflexible individual who will not instigate change when change is necessary. A clear sign of this attitude is his tidy army uniform, which he wears even while riding in the desert, indicating his compulsive, disciplined and formal attitude toward his profession (we never see him out of the uniform).

Initially, it appears that going to war against the Indians and facing the threat of death is the sole way through which Thursday can restore his lost honor. In this sense, Thursday is shown as the kind of hero who, like many other Western and samurai heroes, has no fear of encountering the threat of death.

The hero's conflict can be contextualized in relation to death in battle, for in the classic genres, death and the threat of death against loved ones

Part Two—The Hero's Position and the Theme of Death in Battle

and the ideals of the hero are the final drives toward the expression of the hero's conflicts. This will affect the harmony of the group to which the hero belongs.

In *Fort Apache*, Ford shows the threat of death, directly and visually, when Thursday's daughter Philadelphia (Shirley Temple), on her riding date with a young officer, Mickey O'Rourke (John Agar), finds the dead bodies of two of the fort's soldiers. This is the second type of death[1] according Hagin's ideas (2010, p. 5), which is called "intermediary death." Hagin tells us that "intermediary deaths can be meaningful *in relation to the future*, by being causes of subsequent events." The killing of two soldiers by the Apache Indians is, in effect, the turning point of the film in two ways. First, Thursday has already prophesied that "this is a country for glory." The deaths of the soldiers give him the moral and generic motivation to engage in war with the Indians. Second, the ground on which the Indians have killed the American soldiers now marks the depth of the crisis between American and Indian ideologies and perspectives. The latter are at a disadvantage, for the Indians have killed innocent soldiers. (It should be mentioned that this innocence is from the American political point of view of bygone years, since these soldiers are part of an institution that is involved in killing Indians.) The fact that a virgin couple finds their corpses further emphasizes the purity and the innocence of the dead.

When Thursday is informed of the deaths of the two soldiers, he is determined to avenge their deaths by waging war against the Indians. York disagrees with him because Thursday's scheme could jeopardize the lives of other American soldiers. This "disagreement" is another example of the presence of conflict among the group members.

In this context, the audience witnesses the evolution of the troubled hero's actions in the plot. He has interrupted the order of the system/community/group and, in doing so, has put the lives of the group members in danger. However, I should stress that a troubled hero does not raise the conflict consciously. His emotional issues are part of his character. In *Fort Apache*, early in the film, Thursday admits that he searches for glory and longs for recognition as a victorious commander by the army officials in Washington. His admission explains why he goes to war against the Indians. His reason for fighting the Indians is unique to him; it is not part of the war and political philosophy of the United States. Kitses (2004, p. 69) writes on this matter, "By demonizing the Apache as savage and inferior, Thursday had given himself permission to surpass them in violence and unscrupulous action, while wrapping himself in the banners of duty and glory. Ford ruth-

4. Death, Personal Conflict and Battle

lessly analyzes this process, but by an ideological sleight-of-hand suggests that his behavior was aberrant rather than dominant national policy."

We can apply the principles of this formula to the troubled heroes in Kurosawa's and Leone's films as well. They are trying to prove themselves to their surroundings and, at some point, become obsessed with their quest and lose sight of what is at stake. Kurosawa, in *Kagemusha*,[2] shows us the personal conflicts of a doppelganger/double of Lord Shingen Takeda alongside the lord's son, Katsuyori. Thus, Kurosawa's film juxtaposes two scenarios, which expands on Ford's procedure in *Fort Apache*.

In *Kagemusha*, the leading hero's inner conflict is resolved, while the supporting hero fails to overcome his issues. Both scenarios in this film, or any other film, can affect the functions of death and its subthemes in the plot. It should also be noted that the audience never learns the double's name. This situation never occurs with Ford's heroes, who, due to the generic codes of Westerns and mode of production in Hollywood, are clearly identified with names.

Kagemusha's story narrates the downfall of the Takeda clan, which, in its historical context, led to the emergence of a unified Japan in the 16th century. In its approach to history, this film is similar to Ford's Westerns, in that they pay close attention to the historical myth of the birth of a nation. The theme of death, as discussed in Part One, has a significant role in such an approach, as the hero's death and his memories can contribute to the future of a nation. In *Kagemusha*, an unnamed thief assumes the role of double for Lord Shingen Takeda. The latter soon dies at the hands of an enemy musketeer.[3] This is the film's intermediary death. The double at that point impersonates the lord full-time (Tatsuya Nakadai plays both characters). Meanwhile, Katsuyori (Kenichi Hagiwara), the lord's son, is profoundly frustrated by his political position.

The difference between the double's conflicts and those of Katsuyori is that the latter fails to overcome his emotional issues. His failure later causes an inner-group conflict between himself and the chief retainers of the Takeda clan. The result of such an inner-group conflict is the massacre of Takeda's army. This situation is somewhat similar to *Fort Apache*, in which the actions of a troubled hero cause the deaths of many. The difference is that Thursday, in contrast to Katsuyori, shows awareness of his shortcomings at the hour of death. In addition, as we shall see in the future chapters, Thursday's cult of death will forge constructive memories of him. In *Kagemusha*, due to the annihilation of the Takeda clan, there is no cult of death with which to reproduce a dignified memory of Katsuyori.

Part Two—The Hero's Position and the Theme of Death in Battle

At this point, I will consider the personal conflict of the main hero of Kurosawa's films in relation to the theme of death. Kurosawa, like Ford, usually provides his heroes with a role model, whose actions and thinking teach the hero to get more involved with other people's troubles. In *Seven Samurai*, Kambei Shimada (Takashi Shimura) educates the young hero of the film about the samurai codes of conduct. This kind of hero/shaman (as Campbell would call such a figure) is usually middle aged and experienced in the ways of life. (Ford's father figures fit into a similar category.) In mythology, part of the hero's journey involves following the example of the shaman; the hero, therefore, becomes prudent in his actions under the shaman's tutelage. This development is evident in fiction films too. For instance, in *Kagemusha*, Lord Shingen is the shaman/teacher. The double's primary personal conflict is his fear of death. Kurosawa, in the surrealistic nightmare scene, illustrates the double as being alone, surrounded by thousands of enemies. However, the double overcomes his fear of death as his personality becomes similar to that of the deceased lord. The result of this transformation is the double's involvement in the affairs of the clan/community. Therefore, an outsider engages with a community and its enemies. In doing so, the hero overcomes his inner fears and personal conflicts.

The double triumphs over his shortcomings gradually as he goes through several trials during the film in what Campbell would call his heroic journey. In *Kagemusha*, when Lord Shingen dies, the double at first firmly expresses his lack of devotion to the deceased by saying, "I have no duty to him." However, in the following sequence, observing the lord's burial in the lake motivates the double to continue impersonating Shingen. Following this idea, I argue that for Kurosawa, as with Ford, death and burials are the emotional and moral motivation that directs the hero to his generic characteristics. Hence, in *Kagemusha*, the double's sense of duty awakens as he sees his lord's burial. Prince (1991, p. 281) argues that "as the [double] sees Shingen's burial in Lake Suwa, he is overcome by a conviction that he owes the late lord a profound allegiance that, far from meaningless, has become even more compelling in death." This suggestion is culturally plausible once we remind ourselves of the teachings of Musashi (2012), who explains that the sense of duty and will to die for a moral cause can be found in all classes of the Japanese hierarchical society.

There are two crucial points in the above arguments. First, in Kurosawa's samurai films, if a hero attempts to resolve his emotional issues as part of his life's journey, he embraces one of the essential codes of *bushido*—that is, *giri* (duty). Nitobe (2001, p. 26) writes, "*Giri* primarily meant no more

4. Death, Personal Conflict and Battle

than duty, and I dare say its etymology was derived from the fact, that in our conduct, say to our parents, though love should be the only motive, lacking that there must be some other authority to enforce filial piety, and they formulated this authority in *Giri*." This sense of duty among the samurai in most cases meant following one's lord/superior in death. In his films, Kurosawa does not observe *giri* as limited to the lords or even the warrior class. What is more, Kurosawa shows that all men from different classes have a duty to each other. Human beings are responsible for each other's welfare. Here it can be said that Kurosawa tries to couple the sense of *giri* with humanism, borrowed from western democracy (imported to Japan as an ideological concept during the American occupation following World War II), to which, as suggested by Richie (1984) and Yoshimoto (2000), he was personally sympathetic. During the battle, the hero overcomes his personal demons and, as a result, is more at ease in his role as Lord Shingen's double. Kurosawa referred to this point in one of his interviews (cited in Cardullo, 2008, p. 70): "When we get to the final battle scene, the double watches the death of all these people whose respect he has won and who have won his respect [and he] ... pick[s] up a spear and continue[s] the attack—even after all the others are dead." This explanation is also relevant to the theme of duty and honor in Western films. In Ford's films, as I said before, the deceased moral individuals serve as role models for the future generation. Following a burial, the members of the hero's cult of death (*My Darling Clementine*, *Searchers*, and so on) return to their sense of honor and duty, which is one of the significant aspects of the classic Western hero. In specific instances, when the hero in a Western/samurai film goes through his personal transformation, he comes close to some of the expected norms of heroic conduct in film genre as well as in western and Japanese culture.

Second, similar to Ford's films, for Kurosawa, the locus of war, beyond being the field of death and tragedy, is the place where the hero finds his new mentality/home. Facing the threat of death in battle means that the non-warrior hero is following the same codes of conduct that a samurai hero would. *Bushido* asks the warrior to embrace death with no fear when it is time to die. This is the attitude of the double in *Kagemusha*[4] and Kikuchiyo in *Seven Samurai*. Their deaths stand as proof that although they were not born into a samurai family, at the hour of death they engaged with the same codes of behavior that a real samurai is supposed to embrace. In short, they do not act like cowards or, as I mentioned in the introduction, endure a "dog's death." In the context of the classical Westerns, the hero's death can also show his hidden qualities. Thursday's death proves that he

Part Two—The Hero's Position and the Theme of Death in Battle

is a patriot and a brave commander. The return to his moral codes means that he can be a member of the community/society. Therefore, the battlefield, in most films from Ford and Kurosawa, is the location that enables the hero to become part of society posthumously. Thursday initially interrupts the harmony of the fort; however, his death not only brings social balance back to the fort but also means that he is, in spirit, one of the fort's members. The same can be said about the deceased samurai of the *Seven Samurai*. Their grave forms part of the community, as the villagers bury them in the local cemetery. The living samurai, by contrast, since they are from the warrior class rather than farmers, move on, for they have no fixed position within the social structure of the village.

Leone's heroes, like most of Kurosawa's and some of Ford's protagonists, do not progress socially to become permanent members of a community. The marginal role of the community in Leone's films means that the hero's personal conflict and its relation to the theme of death do not shape the harmony of the society. This is the case because Leone positions the heroes of his films in morally compromising and financially difficult environments. Surviving one's surroundings is the primary goal of these heroes. This theme differs from one of the classic Western features, which would usually assign the hero politically and socially idealistic goals. For example, in the case of Ford's films, Wood (1980, p. 375) argues that the concept of idealistic goals is "rooted in a belief in the development of civilization." As has been said, this outlook is a very significant theme in the Fordian view of American history, as it suggests that the suffering of the current generation will be beneficial to future generations.

In Leone's Westerns, avenging the death of a family member/loved one not only motivates the hero but also marks a severe personal conflict. The outcome of this revenge motif is quite similar to Ford's films. For example, in *For a Few Dollars More*, Colonel Mortimer intends to kill El Indio (Gian Maria Volonte), who has raped his sister. At the film's conclusion, El Indio's death, in line with the conventions of classic films, indicates that the hero (in this case Mortimer) has destroyed the villain. However, in Leone's films, the villain's death, in contrast to classic film traditions, does not necessarily mean the destruction of the evil force. Society remains morally compromised even after the villain dies; there is also no indication that the hero will battle that corruption in the future. Frayling's (2006, p. 160) writings are relevant to my argument: "Leone makes no attempt to engage our sympathy with [his films'] characters, but watches the brutality of his protagonists with a detached calm: they are brutal because of the environment in

4. Death, Personal Conflict and Battle

which they exist. And they make no attempt to change that environment. They accept it, without question." In this sense, it can be concluded that Leone's attitude toward the presence of the corruption and moral decay in society distinguishes his treatment of the Western themes from the old formula of the Western genre.

Furthermore, in terms of the hero's personal conflict, the difference between the films of Leone and those of Ford is that the personal conflict of the former's heroes does not put innocent lives in danger. For example, Leone portrays Mortimer's conflict as he remembers his sister's death constantly throughout the film. Although this personal issue motivates him to stand up to the villain, it does not escalate into an obstacle that distracts him from his main goal. By contrast, if seeking vengeance only motivates the hero and does not create any personal conflict for him, it can be a threat to those around him. The "others" are not a community or a small group; they are the hero's only friends. However, this friendship is an unstable relationship, for friends, in Leone's films, place their self-interest ahead of the other person's welfare. For example, in *The Good, the Bad and the Ugly*, Tuco (Eli Wallach) seeks revenge against Blondie (Clint Eastwood) for having double-crossed him. This is a puzzling thought, as these two characters are allies. Their supposed friendship, as Kitses (2004, p. 257) suggests, is "a product of need rather than commitment." It is therefore likely that the two friends will betray each other's trust and even threaten each other's lives. Kitses' further comment (2004, p. 268) goes on to explain, "Friendship on Leone's frontier is as unstable a relationship as other forms of alliance. In this, it appears a more flexible and complex bond, more 'realistic' than conventional notions allow, in that it can accommodate both respect and warmth, however unspoken, as well as lies and betrayals." Kitses' comments make sense in relation to the narcissistic ethos of Leone's male character. Tuco is angry because, as he says, "No one double-crosses Tuco." Therefore, although Leone's characters do not follow many of the generic conventions that Ford's heroes do, they have their own personal code of conduct. In the case of *The Good, the Bad and the Ugly*, Blondie violates Tuco's code; as a consequence, the latter intends to lead the former into a desert to kill him. Blondie escapes the threat of death only when a stagecoach arrives carrying wounded and dead soldiers. This is the turning point of the film. Tuco learns the name of a cemetery where Carson has hidden the army's stolen gold; Blondie likewise determines the name of the grave in which Carson has buried the gold. In this sequence, Leone provides the main heroes with a mutual new goal—that is, pursuing a bigger fortune rather than chasing

Part Two—The Hero's Position and the Theme of Death in Battle

tiny amounts of money, as the two do in the earlier section of the film. In an ironic sense, the quest for gold restores their former friendship. Male friendship is certainly part of Ford's and Kurosawa's films as well. Nevertheless, since Leone's films are less centered on issues of community, national ideology and redeeming romance, male friendship appears to be more pronounced on screen compared to the films of Ford and Kurosawa.

In Leone's films, once an outside force projects the threat of death (similar to Ford's and Kurosawa's characters), the friends/rivals unite against the common enemy—for example, both Blondie and Tuco stand up to Angel Eyes, who is their mutual enemy. In *The Good, the Bad and the Ugly*, Leone provides the audience with the background story of one of the two heroes—namely, Tuco. In the scene in the Catholic mission, it is revealed that Tuco is from a poor farming background. He failed to earn a living as a farmer, which is why he has become a bandit. His desire for money has grown to such an extent that he puts his own life in jeopardy with the law and bounty hunters. His conflict with his past life contributes immensely to the friendship (and therefore unity) between Tuco and Blondie, since Tuco's impoverished upbringing has created a sense of avarice in him, and Blondie has a greedy nature as well. This is shown early in the film when they attempt to double-cross each other. However, their mutual desire to reach their goal means that greed is part of their characterization. This ethos of Leone's heroes is not a situation that is conducive to redemption.

The hero's journey in Leone's work does not mean that, after facing the threat of death, the hero will transform from a fortune-seeking individual into, for example, a law-abiding citizen. In fact, the journey rationalizes the hero's morals and goals. This situation can be seen in the light of the previously mentioned point that Leone's visual texts are more concerned with tangible physical action, rather than dwelling too profoundly on the clash of moralities. This is so because his films view the hero's inner conflict on a personal level, not in a national ideological sense. Still, there are moments when Leone shows, even for a brief time, the larger clash. Blondie offers his view on war (after witnessing the massacre of the Northern and Southern soldiers on the battlefield) by saying, "I've never seen so many lives wasted so badly." This depoliticized view can mean that in Leone's film (like Ford's and Kurosawa's works), the battlefield is the place where the hero's ideological position is challenged. In Leone's film, Blondie and Tuco (and even Angel Eyes) are educated about the futility of a large-scale war once they encounter the horrors of civil war. This can be seen in parallel to Frayling's comment (2008, p. 50) that "to the three main characters in

4. Death, Personal Conflict and Battle

this story, the Civil War is a bloody and dangerous distraction." It is true that these three characters are bandits and bounty hunters; facing the threat of death and killing others is the reality of their vocation. Nevertheless, war and destruction in this film illustrate these characters' humane side. The omnipresence of death in a war-torn America distracts these characters, even if only for short intervals, from their personal issues (namely, their self-centered fortune-seeking nature). This argument is relevant in the case of Ford's and Kurosawa's heroes as well, since they also put aside their interests (financially or romantic) once facing outsiders who threaten the well-being of innocent people or communities. The visual signs of this sacrifice of the hero in the films of Leone are found in moments like when Angel Eyes comes across a group of wounded soldiers (and, in contrast to his supposed evil nature, helps a severely injured soldier), or when Tuco and Blondie witness the deaths of thousands of young men. Their wooden, intense facial expressions relax, albeit only for a short while, and their faces become vulnerable and humane. Thus, the battlefield in Leone's work, similar to that of Ford and Kurosawa, is the hero's place of transformation. However, this change, in the case of Leone's hero, is momentary and does not reform him for the better.

5
Death, Group Conflict and Battle

The inner-group conflict is the clash of attitudes among individuals who are members of the same group (e.g., fellow travelers, friends, colleagues, family members, and so on). Nevertheless, differences in their social status, sense of morality, goals and methods for reaching those goals can create conflict. The group dynamics are a significant aspect of Western and samurai films, for, beyond showing the position of the hero in relation to wider society, they also reveal the social attitudes toward historical change. For example, in *Stagecoach*, conflict is visible between different sets of social class and ideology that two of the stagecoach passengers represent and express. On the one hand, Mrs. Mallory's traditional, courteous, yet arrogant behavior represents the Southern aristocratic and conservative ethics. In contrast, Dallas portrays more liberal attitudes, which the west symbolizes. Facing the threat of death in battle (as the Apache Indians are charging against the stagecoach and its passengers), however, eliminates these social and class differences—at least for the battle period. During battle scenes, action-based films often oblige group members, despite their differences, to face a common enemy and its destructive morality. Samurai films have similar codes that bind the members of a group to unite against a mutual enemy.

In Western and samurai films, the hero who is responsible for the conflict in the group frequently faces objections from the members of the group to which he belongs. In *Fort Apache*, Captain York is the primary voice of this objection. Ford initially portrays York as a peace-seeking officer in contrast to Thursday's character. York avoids war if possible; however, this avoidance is not due to his lack of courage in facing death. Once engaged in battle, he is a brave fighter, risking his life to help the wounded American soldiers. In fact, similar to Doc Boone in *Stagecoach*, York is the protector of life. That is why, in following his personal code, he sees Thursday's fight with Indians as an unnecessary venture, for it endangers the lives of many others. This type of hero, in the context of the theme of death and its subcategories, has a positive attitude toward the cycle of life and contributes

5. Death, Group Conflict and Battle

immensely to its formation. In *Fort Apache*, during the heat of the battle with the Indians toward the end of the film, and recognizing the impending defeat, York sends Mickey away to safety and shouts at him, "Marry that girl!" (Philadelphia). This, as Darby (2006, p. 85) writes, is one of Ford's motifs regarding securing the future of the American nation: "When Captain York ... sends Mickey for help, we see another thematic point much stressed in *Fort Apache* and elsewhere in Ford's Westerns: the need for people to sacrifice (their happiness or lives, if it is needed) to ensure a better future for an oncoming generation (whether already present or implicitly to come)." York's romantic instruction melds with Ford's attitude to military service: marriage guarantees continuity of the institutions that sustain America, in terms of both giving birth to the next generation and protecting against external threats. Toward the end of the film, the presence of his young son emphasizes Mickey's contribution to the future of the cavalry.

Once the troubled hero dies, the supporting hero will function as the representative of his cult of death. Thus, death resolves the conflict among the group members. This situation can be problematic when we remind ourselves of the personal issues of the fallen hero. A clear example is the ending of *Fort Apache*. At least upon the first viewing, the conclusion appears to contradict the rest of the film. For much of their time together, York and Thursday are in constant conflict; however, in the last two minutes of the film, York appears to be confident of Thursday's leadership for a superior society, the two qualities that the late commander appeared to lack. Wood (1980, p. 380) has this to say regarding the complexity of this film's ending: "Although the film has proved Thursday wrong all along the line, the ending performs an abrupt *volte-face*." I argue that perhaps Wood sees the ending and the conclusion of this cinematic text as similar concepts (hence his comment about the *volte-face*).

Barbara Herrnstein Smith has a different view regarding film endings and conclusions. Neupert (1995, p. 13) writes on her theory:

> [Smith] distinguishes between "endings" and "conclusions," writing that any event, narrative or otherwise, may simply stop or end; only a text or artwork may *conclude*, with the conclusion coming at a definite "termination point." She writes, "closure may be regarded as a modification of structure that makes *stasis*, or the absence of further continuation, the most probable succeeding event." Thus, for Smith, endings are judged by their appropriateness to the overall structure and the narrated events or context.

Smith's idea is somewhat related to my theory that the happy conclusion of *Fort Apache* (in which York is promoted to colonel, Mickey and Philadel-

Part Two—The Hero's Position and the Theme of Death in Battle

phia are married, and the amateur private at the film's beginning is now an experienced sergeant major), rather than its ending, is due to the successful forging of the mythical cult of death. As a result, this element of the film's conclusion can make sense in relation to the rest of film. To explain this point in depth, I shall analyze the sequence in which Thursday tries to sit on his new armchair in his house and compare this scene to the ending sequence of the film in which the audience witnesses his mythical cult of death whitewashing his actions.

There are few interesting scenes in the first sequence that demand explanation. Before Thursday sits, for a moment he glances at the framed portrait of Abraham Lincoln on the wall. Considering Lincoln's legendary position in American history and political vernacular, this portrait, in the context of death, carries a symbolic meaning. Ford here foreshadows Thursday's fate: he will die and, in death, become a legend. This begs a further question: How does this transition happen within the context of death in the case of any troubled hero? The transition occurs through the formation of the mythical cult of death. Thursday's actions have caused conflict in the group consisting of his family and the fort community. Nevertheless, when he is dead, the inhabitants of the fort act as the members of his cult of death, which creates a legend out of the deceased hero's life. Another question is this: How does Ford suggest the possibility of dying and becoming a legend? In my view, he suggests this idea through his portrayal of the hero's shortcomings and failings. In *Fort Apache*, the chair incident is such a portrayal. In Ford's narratives, a chair and the act of a hero sitting on it is a motif. In *My Darling Clementine*, for example, Wyatt Earp tries to sit on the chair in the barber shop. Unfortunately, the chair breaks. However, he manages to keep his balance on the chair thanks to the help of his brothers (family support) and the barber (community support). In *Fort Apache*, once Thursday's chair breaks there is no one to aid him, and he falls comically to the ground. His daughter (family) and the maid (given by the community to Thursday's household) are absent. They only come to his aid when he is already on the ground. In this way, the film indicates fact that Thursday, after all, is human. This scene can also be a reference to the evolution of Thursday's character from an unloved commander to a legendary figure. The family and community are in conflict with Thursday and are unable to save him from his downfall and potential death. However, they will help him once he has failed, so that his memory survives thanks to the cult of death.

The above observations are related to the closing sequence of the film,

5. Death, Group Conflict and Battle

in which York, previously the voice of objection, becomes a representative of the dead hero's cult of death. As the new commander of the fort, he promotes the false memories of the late Colonel Thursday to a visiting press group from Washington. This reading is based on the three alterations in York's character. First, his attire in this sequence (in contrast to his informal style at the beginning of the film) has changed to a formal and disciplined army uniform. Hence, on a sartorial level, he has come closer to Thursday than he really was. The second alteration is York's political attitude toward war with the Indians: he is no longer a pacifist. Thursday's death functions as the trigger for that change, which brings York in line with the political priorities of the American nation, his generic status as a Western hero and, ultimately, enlightenment regarding what is really at stake—namely, that violent outsiders, like Apache Indians, have the potential to damage the peace and order of American society. Therefore, York, as the commander of the fort, stops negotiating with the Indians and speaks about fighting them to make the frontier a safer place for the America.

At this point, Thursday's cult of death is experiencing duality. This duality establishes the contrast between social duty (suggested by York's deeds) and personal glory (indicated by Thursday's actions). The cult is half-historical in that York follows Thursday's example by waging war against the Indians. However, Thursday's cult of death is also half-mythical, as York manipulates the truth about the deceased's actions. York convinces the reporters from Washington that he is fighting Indians like Thursday, with the intention of expanding the frontier. This statement means that York's agenda with the Indians is an ideological one—to better American society. However, Thursday went to battle against the Apaches for personal reasons, not ideological ones. York speaks about forcing the Apache Indians back to reservation camps and bringing safety to the frontier. These were not Thursday's concerns. He was pursuing glory. He sought to prove to himself (and to the officials who sent him to the fort) that he was still a victorious commander.

The third and final alteration made to York's mentality can be seen in the lies that he foists upon the reporters after Thursday's death. He tells them how accounts of Thursday's glories are "true to every detail." He also keeps Thursday's saber in his office and has the dead commander's framed portrait on the wall. In this scene, there is a symmetry with the beginning: Thursday had a framed portrait of a legend (Lincoln) on his wall, while York has a portrait of another legend (as the reporters suggest)—Thursday—on his wall. Lincoln's portrait functions as a symbol for the nation,

Part Two—The Hero's Position and the Theme of Death in Battle

whereas the portrait of Thursday is a symbol of group identity for the fort's inhabitants. Incidentally, Thursday's portrait is much bigger than Lincoln's. This means that the mythical cult is fully forged and shaped. Darby's writings (2006, pp. 89–90) can be linked to my argument: "Thursday's concern with historical glory is aptly rewarded by the framed portrait of him that decorates York's wall in the film's final sequence. Thursday has become more impressive in the painting than he ever was in life." Ford showed the birth of Lincoln as an American legend in *Young Mr. Lincoln* (1939). In this film, Lincoln is a humble lawyer who intends to prove the innocence of two brothers accused of murder. In *Fort Apache*, he has become a legendary role model for a troubled hero who wages an unnecessary war. In life, Lincoln revolutionized the political and social culture of America. He was a founding father of the Republican Party and ended the Civil War (1861–1865) in victory for the Union, ending slavery in the process. In death, he became a legend for what he did in life; his cult of death is a historical one. Thursday, by contrast, dies in defeat, but a mythical cult of death elevates him to the status of a legend.

The heroic (and mostly false) account of a commander's/soldier's life is an aspect of war culture. Paul Virilio, in *War and Cinema: The Logistics of Perception* (1989, p. 39), writes on this matter, "Dr. Gustave Le Bon wrote in 1916, 'War touches not only the material life but also the thinking of nations ... and here we meet again the basic notion that it is not the rational which manages the world but forces of effective, mystical or collective origin which guide men. The seductive promptings of these mystical formulas are all the more powerful in that they remain rather ill defined ... immaterial forces are the true steerers of combat.'" One significant point here is that forging the mythical cult of death is a characteristic of the victorious side of the war (Thursday loses the battle, but, at the end, the America wins the war against the Indians). Victors motivated by their victory will try to shed a brighter light on their personal shortcomings.

The mythical cult has another function beyond creating false memories of the late hero: it maintains the morale of the group members. At the end of *Fort Apache*, the soldiers become professionals in their vocation. This is evident in York's line when he says that Thursday "made them better soldiers." As the editor of the Shinbone newspaper suggests at the end of *The Man Who Shot Liberty Valance*, "When a fact becomes a legend, publish the legend."

Unlike most of the heroes of Ford's early Westerns, Kurosawa's heroes stand up to various political/social issues. In most cases, they are not on the winning side in a financial or sexual sense. This means that Kurosawa's

5. Death, Group Conflict and Battle

hero will often lose the actual war (e.g., in *Kagemusha*). In some cases (more akin to Ford's later works, such as *The Man Who Shot Liberty Valance* and *7 Women*), Kurosawa's hero helps the community to win one battle but still cannot be part of that community, because aspects of his morality are at odds with the norms of the community (e.g., *Sanjuro* and *Seven Samurai*).

Since Kurosawa's heroes meet a different fate than Ford's regarding prosperity, there is no reason for the mythical cult of death to manipulate the facts about the hero's personal shortcomings. In fact, in some cases (contrary to Ford) Kurosawa's troubled heroes are not redeemed for their shortcomings. In this case, if the troubled samurai dies, the cult of death is divided and ambivalent regarding how to remember the deceased (as in *Rashomon*). In the rest of Kurosawa's films, a historical cult of death honors the memory of the troubled hero. The lack of a mythical cult of death means that there will be no misrepresentation of the facts after the demise of the conflict's advocate. For example, in *Kagemusha*, Katsuyori, who advocates for battle (like Colonel Thursday in *Fort Apache*), sees victory on the battlefield as the sole way for others to recognize his worth. Unfortunately, Katsuyori only achieves death and destruction; therefore, there is no cult of death for him in the film.

I have already argued that romance does not have a significant function within the cinematic texts of Kurosawa. As a result, in most of his films, the absence of romance culminates in the supporting hero's moral ossification. Such a hero can find no way to return to the generic obligations of the samurai film. In *Kagemusha*, this means that the hero's personal issues bring him into direct conflict with other retainers. They are the voices of dissent, as they are against marching into an unnecessary war. Nonetheless, out of commitment to their superior, the retainers accompany him to war under any circumstances.

In Kurosawa's samurai films, when the hero does not overcome obstacles, including his own conflicts, both he and the group/community he belongs to are destroyed (as in *Kagemusha*). In the latter category, the retainers are fully aware that Katsuyori's plans for the war will lead to their demise. Yet an old retainer encourages others to go to war by saying, "Soon, we will be with Lord Shingen." They follow Katsuyori out of their sense of *giri* to the clan. They protest verbally against his actions, but at the time of battle, they accompany him nevertheless. This is quite similar to Ford's films. No matter how grave and profound the inner-group conflict is, the group members stand together in facing an adversary. They follow the classic Western code of duty that obliges them to be loyal to their group/community.

Part Two—The Hero's Position and the Theme of Death in Battle

In *Kagemusha*, however, the audience witnesses a scenario absent from Ford's films—due to the death of the entire community, there will be no cult of death within the diegesis of the plot to remember the Takeda clan. This lack, as we shall see later, influences the ideological attitude of the film. For now, it suffices to say that this setting is different from Ford's films, in which, even if the main hero dies, there is always a cult of death honoring his memory. In these films, the cult of death is a sign that most of the film's characters have survived the threat of death. They can enjoy the prosperity that is the result of expanding westward and fighting external forces (e.g., criminals, Indians). On the opposite side of the cinematic/cultural spectrum, in Kurosawa's works, if there is a cult of death, its members will only learn a lesson of morality rather than achieving romantic/financial gain. This point is evident in the conclusion of *Seven Samurai* when the three remaining samurai leave the village. In terms of family bliss and financial success, they do not achieve anything. However, they are enlightened regarding their own profession and lifestyle: "the winners are those farmers, not us," admits the older of the samurai. Following the defeat of the bandits, the villagers can return to their settled and somewhat content lifestyle (they are dancing and singing in unison while working in the rice fields); in contrast, the remaining warriors, physically and emotionally exhausted, leave the village without any idealistic change in their lives. Richie (1996, p. 103) emphasizes this point by writing that the old samurai "hoped to win, and further had hoped that this winning would somehow change something." The ending of the film teaches him and his companions that since they cannot change their way of life, they should leave the village.

Although scholars such as Richie and Yoshimoto have labeled *Seven Samurai* a Western film, I see the film's conclusion as a departure from the Western genre. In most of Ford's works, for example, the leading male hero, beyond defeating the villain, creates a family; he becomes part of a conventional social group. In Kurosawa's opus, in the rare instance of a romantic subplot, the action and romance sections of the narrative move in parallel with each other, never meeting. In most Western films (including the works of Ford, Hawks, and Mann), the greater part of the community will survive, and the death of the fallen hero (or heroes) is an ideological guideline that motivates others to follow this actual or mythical example. Those heroes who learned this lesson (like Mickey, York, Ringo, Philadelphia, Dallas, and so on) will be rewarded with a family and/or a higher professional position. Kurosawa circumvents this kind of Western ending. Instead, he moves toward the conclusion that those characters who have survived the threat of death are aware of the past mistakes of the dead hero.

In Leone's films, in contrast to those of Ford and Kurosawa, more than witnessing groups, the audience sees self-serving characters who form a volatile temporary association to respond to the threats of a mutual enemy out of need. In *The Good, the Bad and the Ugly*, the three main characters, motivated to find the gold coins that belong to the army, form alliances with each other or against each other (Tuco and Blondie against Angel Eyes, Blondie and Angel Eyes against Tuco). The three men are not a group in the traditional sense that the audience would come across in the films of Ford or Kurosawa. Nevertheless, the trio is the closest entity to the idea of the group in this film.

The way this togetherness responds to the threat of outside forces is different from how the members of a group/community would react to the external threat in Ford's Westerns. In Leone's West, fighting with the external forces does not resolve the conflict between Blondie and Tuco, but it will affect the dynamics of the inner-group conflict between them. The main reason for this scenario is that Leone's films, in general, do not partake of the idealistic morality found in the works of Ford and Mann. In *The Good, the Bad and the Ugly*, however, the three main characters of the film have similar experiences with the American Civil War. They encounter the horrors of war repeatedly on their quest for gold. Encountering so many massacres positions them on a journey that informs them of the depth of the tragedies of war. In this film, the American Civil War is the wasteland that the hero should overcome. When, as part of the film's conclusion, the main characters face each other in the now-celebrated standoff, their experience with war, and what they have learned from it (if anything), does not motivate them to change their goal. Therefore, none of the three main characters acknowledges the internal conflict of their alliances.

Furthermore, the above idea of learning takes a form different from Ford's and Kurosawa's films. None of Leone's characters fall in love (Ford's education strategy) or learn a valuable moral lesson that will resolve or address the internal conflict (Kurosawa). As a result, Leone's heroes do not contribute directly to the welfare of society (the point of learning in Ford's and Kurosawa's films). They realize that their initial goal—to survive their surrounding environment—is a rational choice, evidenced by their continual search for the army gold.

Additionally, in Leone's films (in contrast to Ford's and Kurosawa's films), none of the main characters object to the deeds of the hero with the

Part Two—The Hero's Position and the Theme of Death in Battle

personal conflict because these characters have the same goal. In *The Good, the Bad and the Ugly*, a minor supporting character, Tuco's brother, who is a Catholic priest, objects to the bandit's actions. He is a judgmental person who condemns Tuco's actions. However, his criticism of the bandit's lifestyle is not implicitly valid regarding Leone's treatment of the genre; after all, becoming a bandit is the only available option for Tuco to survive political and social hardships. In this instance, the difference between Ford's and Leone's approaches to religion is quite clear. In Ford's films, Christianity is primarily valued for social cohesion rather than doctrine—it is a social force bringing people together rather than an organized structure that aims to govern and control their lives. In Leone's work, by contrast, religion is a concept capable of separating two siblings.

The above points mean that, for Leone, a hero's conflict is not necessarily a negative characteristic that leads to inner-group conflict. In fact, it can contribute to the hero's survival. For example, in *A Fistful of Dollars*, the innkeeper constantly complains about the anonymous hero's avaricious nature. This, however, is not a damaging personal conflict, but rather an essential approach if the hero wishes to survive the hardships around him. This desire for money becomes the hero's strategy for manipulating the two rival gangs in San Miguel for his personal gain.

In Leone's films, as the narrative progresses, male friendship may reduce the level of disagreement. At the end of *The Good, the Bad and the Ugly*, Blondie leaves Tuco with no horse and a rope around his neck in Sadhill cemetery. The two are again playing their tricks from earlier in the film; the only difference is that the villain has been killed. However, in a way, seeking the fortune enriches their friendship. That is why Blondie, in contrast to the beginning of the film, does not rob Tuco of his share of the money. This final irony shows the attitude toward death in Leone's Western films. In Ford, once the villain is dead, the hero survives the threat of death. This is not the case in Leone's narrative, where the threat of death is constant. Thus, Ford's films suggest that, at some point, law and order will prevail in the community/society; in Leone's films, however, the constant presence of the threat of death means that forces of evil are too powerful to be overcome by the civic progress of society.

6

Death, External Conflict and Battle

The external conflict springs from the ideologically stigmatized actions of a force that is outside of the community and its value system. In Ford's films, the source of external conflict is usually the individuals or groups that represent the "others" who declare war on the hero and his ethics (the ideology of the others is harmful to a peaceful community). Furthermore, the others' sense of morality endangers the lives and honor of innocent people (along with the overall well-being of a civilized community). In contrast to the opposing force, the hero's actions have positive impacts on the community/group/society, since he stands up to the evil acts of the outsiders.

The Indians in most classic Westerns function as representatives of primitive ethics that can and will harm the peace and order of the said civilized community/society. Wood (in Caughie, 1981, p. 89) explains the general position of the Indians in Western films: "Indians in Westerns are not just a people but a concept; they have a basic mythic meaning on which individual directors bring many changes but which remains an underlying constant. As savages, they represent the wild, the untamed, the disruptive, the vital forces that remain largely inassimilable into any civilization man has so far elaborated." In short, the Indians' ideology does not integrate with that of white America. Besides, in classic Western films, the actions of Indians result in the destruction of innocent white individuals and their way of life. The Indians are thus a threat to "us" (i.e., the intended audience's surrogates).

In the case of *Fort Apache*, Ford justifies the fight against the Indians by portraying them as embodying a savage culture that threatens the safety of the American people. *Fort Apache*'s opening credits sequence suggests this dichotomy: Here the American soldiers are sitting on their horses in disciplined military formation, their sabers sheathed, suggesting that the American army avoids unnecessary violence. By representing the American soldiers in this fashion, Ford indicates that the American army equals order

Part Two—The Hero's Position and the Theme of Death in Battle

and perfection. As Will Wright, in *Sixguns and Society* (1977, p. 86), postulates on the function of the cavalry in Westerns, "When a Western plot is about professional fighters like a cavalry 'How the fight is fought' is now the crucial issue, since the fight itself generates the values that replace the values of the society in the myth." The visual representation of the cavalry in the opening title sequence explains how the "fight is fought"—in a civilized manner, and as a last resort, for the army is a sophisticated harmonious union. This scene then cuts to a dance in the fort (as the names of the film's stars appear on screen), where Thursday is dancing alongside Sergeant Major O'Rourke's wife. This arrangement indicates a sense of harmony within the life of the regiment. However, Thursday later threatens this balance through his prejudice against O'Rourke (Ward Bond) and his family due to O'Rourke being a noncommissioned officer.

An image York riding in the Mexican desert follows this part of the opening credits. Later in the film, Ford provides more details about this journey, in which an American officer endured the harsh environment of the desert to find the Apache Indians in order to make peace with them and bring them back to their homeland. The representation of the Americans once again indicates their peace-making ethos.

According to the above points, it can be said that the opening credits have created three ideological meanings for the American cavalry: (a) they are disciplined; (b) they live in synchronicity in the fort; and (c) although they face the threat of death (as they are soldiers), they are seeking order and peace, not death. Ford challenges these principles throughout the film, as Thursday obsessively pursues war when it is not altogether justified. However, in the end, Thursday's death brings discipline and harmony back into the fort, as the entire community unites in the next battle against the Indians. A unified fort is not about killing Indians but about winning the west and establishing law and order in the country.

Moreover, for Ford, the Indians are split into two groups: the savage Indians who bring mayhem, destruction and damage to civilization (e.g., the Apache Indians in *Stagecoach*) and the civilized Indians who want to live in peace with others and carry on their ancient traditions (e.g., the Indians in *Cheyenne Autumn* [1964]). The opening credits of *Fort Apache* conceptualize the Indians as one threatening entity. They are shown carrying weapons, suggesting that they seek violence. There is also no dance scene featuring the Indians—their harmony is rooted in violence and promoting death. In classic Western films where there is a dance scene involving Indians, it is usually part of a war ritual. In *Fort Apache*, the Indians'

6. Death, External Conflict and Battle

presence in the opening credits is accompanied by non-diegetic, intense orchestral music like that in the opening of *Stagecoach*. *Fort Apache* deals with the same external threat as the earlier film. Thus, the cavalry should fight the Indians to keep the frontier safe from harm. Although the American cavalry is made up of trained warriors, they seek violence only when facing the violent actions of the Apaches. This suggests another possible meaning for the battlefield—it is the location where noble and savage face each other. Once the heroes challenge these corrupt values, there will be a free space to cultivate and nurture new civilized attitudes.

The next point is that in most Western films, the threat of death raised by external forces results in the enlightenment and emotional maturity of a leading or supporting hero. As I have explained in the introduction, Hagin (2010, pp. 12–13) suggests that the death of film characters in classical films imparts new information to the audience, since, at the hour of their death, an individual can demonstrate their real strength and worth. A hero thus has one last chance to acknowledge his shortcomings or past mistakes. This acknowledgment resolves the internal conflict within the group that the hero belongs to; forging the cult of death is the sign of this resolution.

In *Fort Apache*, Ford shows the hero's acknowledgment of his shortcomings toward the end of the climactic battle. The first visual sign of Thursday's modified awareness is that he takes York's horse and saber to go back to battle and rejoin what remains of his platoon. Borrowing York's weapon and transport indicates that Thursday has begun to adopt aspects of the latter's persona. This new prudence shows itself in the ensuing line, when Thursday orders York (before York's departure), "When you command this regiment, command it." In short, be firm and strong in your decisions. York, as the new commander of the regiment, will also be in command of the community. After all, the community resides in an army fort. The same social harmony that was disturbed by Thursday's actions will be restored as York engages in battle with the Indians at the end of the film. Thursday's death is the trigger that brings the fort's inhabitants back to their generic and social obligations since, before Thursday's death, they were not fully committed to war with outsiders.

I further argue that the field of war is the place where the enlightenment of the fallen hero happens. Thus, in a way, Thursday deserves the posthumous recognition. The battlefield is also where the transformation of the supporting hero has occurred. Here I am referring to the fact that, as York adopts aspects of Thursday's persona, his actions become similar to that of the fallen commander. Kitses (2004, p. 63) writes that, by the end

Part Two—The Hero's Position and the Theme of Death in Battle

of the film, York "has not only inherited the command and accepted the necessity of falsifying the truth of Thursday's action, but he has also taken on Thursday's role in making war on the Apache." This change marks York's enlightenment regarding the war with Indians, in which he will face the threat of death. There is a visual reference to this threat in the way that the regiment leaves the fort at the end of the film in the same way that it went to battle under the command of Thursday—women and children are on the balconies and worried, but they see their men off with pride.

The second sign of the recognition of one's mistakes is seen when Thursday returns to his remaining men. He apologizes to them; because of this admission of guilt, perhaps the deceased hero deserves his mythical cult of death that preserves the ethics and moralities of the community. Sergeant O'Rourke (Mickey's father) acknowledges the commander's change of attitude as they are about to be killed by the Indians when he tells Thursday to "keep your apologies for our grandchildren." Thursday's silence when O'Rourke utters this line is suggestive, as it could be his way of consenting to his daughter marrying Mickey O'Rourke. In life, the dynamics between Thursday and O'Rourke did not work, since the former snubbed the latter for not being part of the regular army. After Thursday's death, this aspect of the group conflict is resolved. Regular officers and noncommissioned officers all fall on the same ground.

The result of Thursday's supposed blessing of Mickey and Philadelphia's marriage is that he contributes to the cycle of life and the continuity of social morals. In death, he has become the typical Fordian hero who leaves a positive mark on the future of the community. Ford's depiction of Philadelphia's fate emphasizes this point. The last time the audience sees her on screen, she is married to Mickey and has become a mother. Her garments at the beginning of the film were of the East Coast style; by the end, they have changed. She wears the conventional, yet practical, clothes of a married woman of the west, which indicates that she has become part of the community. She has also contributed to the life of the fort through giving birth to a son, which, in the masculine and militaristic atmosphere of the fort, means a potential soldier. Philadelphia's son carries on the legacy of his two dead grandfathers and the living commander: his name is Michael Thursday York O'Rourke. This child has become the symbol of the past, giving new life to the present (and most likely the future) of the regiment and its potential achievements and exploitations. As McBride (2003, p. 457) observes, "Michael Thursday York O'Rourke is a living embodiment of memory, tradition, and the future." Thus, the deaths of the moral Americans

6. Death, External Conflict and Battle

are not futile. Their place of burial, which was the wasteland that the hero entered, is now won over and will be expanded by the present and future generations. Therefore, even in death the fallen soldiers contributed to building the utopia that is America. This is similar to the message in Ford's pre-war-era Westerns, most notably *My Darling Clementine*.

In Kurosawa's films as well, the villains are usually outsiders who have a different ideology compared to that of the main group. In some of his films (as in Ford's films), these outsiders initiate the battle and its subsequence violence. The samurai codes of honor and conduct, as conceptualized in *bushido*, continuously ask the warriors to challenge the immoral outsiders as part of their duty to their lord and the clan/community they serve. There are also cases in Kurosawa's films (though based on a different cultural-generic motivation than what is observed in Ford's films[1]) in which the hero/heroes are not part of the community. Due to two distinct reasons—either samurai codes of honor or financial obligation—the heroes help the community battle the bandits/villains. A clear example of this arrangement is seen in *Seven Samurai* (1954), where poor villagers hire a group of the samurai (moral outsiders) to help them fight the bandits (the corrupt outsiders). The way Kurosawa portrays the bandits in *Seven Samurai* is like Ford's exhibition of the Indians, as he strips the villains of their individuality. Ford's cavalry trilogy—*Rio Grande* (1950), *Fort Apache* and *She Wore a Yellow Ribbon* (1949)—depicts the Indians as an antagonistic force, which the Americans should face for the sake of future white American generations. Both filmmakers treat the external forces as a collective that challenges the heroes' physical and emotional strength.

Moreover, like Ford, Kurosawa is interested in the historical and ideological process of the emergence of a nation. The difference is that Ford is mainly concerned with the victorious side, whereas Kurosawa often dwells more on the losing side (which are those samurai who were marginalized in Japanese society rather than the members of the samurai class who prosper in Japanese society), along with its moral position and the lessons that can be learned from its downfall. Such a learning process is featured in most samurai films. As Thornton (2008) suggests, in these films, the heroes are most likely tragic figures, for they lose their family and social prestige. Kurosawa's *Kagemusha* merits study regarding the relationship between the theme of death and external conflict, as there are thematic similarities between this film's conclusion and the conclusion of Ford's cavalry films, most notably *Fort Apache*.

The role of outsiders as those who initiate the external conflict is also

Part Two—The Hero's Position and the Theme of Death in Battle

part of samurai films. Due to the political system of medieval Japan, in samurai films that are concerned with Japanese history, the enemy will be other clans within the Japanese social and political system. Their attitudes and ethics clash with those of the hero and the community to which he belongs (or tries to defend). In the case of films such as *Kagemusha* and *Ran*, the outside force is a rival clan/family faction inspired by historical accounts. These films inform the audience of different ideological and political attitudes that may have been involved in the shaping of Japanese history. For example, in *Kagemusha*, Kurosawa devotes many scenes to depicting the main enemies of the Takeda clan—the historical figures Oda Nobunaga (1534–1582) and Tokugawa Ieyasu (1543–1616).

That said, I also consider the case of criminals as outsiders in samurai films. Usually, these bandits appear in the same fashion as criminals/Indians in Western films: namely, they are a collective force. Their actions harm small communities, such as the farming village in *Seven Samurai*. These bandits have roots in Japanese history since they are usually *ronin* who have gone rogue.

Similar to Westerns, in samurai films the villains' actions and values bring destruction to the community's social fabric. In *Kagemusha*, Kurosawa initially portrays an attitude similar to Ford's approach to battle. In this sense, I argue that the battlefield is the place where a nation can be forged. The shared concern between the two genres positions death as an element that can contribute to building the future of the larger society. Also, in the films of Ford and Kurosawa, the main or supporting hero does not initially approve of such an attitude. Part of that character's journey is that, by the end of the film, he has reached the same conclusion about the importance of war and death for the emergence of the nation.

In *Kagemusha*'s opening sequence, a long take shows Lord Shingen, the thief and Shingen's brother (his former double). Kurosawa presents both the lord and the thief as people familiar with the concept of death. The thief accuses Shingen of being a warmonger whose actions have resulted in the deaths of many. The lord does not deny this assertion. In fact, he argues that war is necessary to unify the country. He points out that without the civil war, "there will be more mountains of the dead" in the country. Therefore, from Shingen's point of view, death is not only a social reality but also a political necessity for the good of the nation. Such a view sees beyond the codes of the warrior class that promote facing the threat of death in battle with honor and considers it a political motivation to forge a unified community. This point is important, for when Shingen is dead

6. Death, External Conflict and Battle

his political and historical ideology functions as an invisible force within the film's story. His enemies also should win the war in order to unite the country. The forging of a nation depends on such a mentality.

However, the double has just survived the threat of death through the interference of Lord Shingen's brother, Nobukado. This double is a criminal who, as Shingen puts it, "has probably killed someone," referring to the thief's possibly violent nature. Yoshimoto (2000, p. 351) writes the following about this scene: "The thief was rescued when he was about to be executed publicly, so that to some extent when he meets Shingen, he is not alive. Symbolically, the thief is already dead." This symbolic death of the hero means that he is separated from his former self—his old community—and is reaching a new self, a new community, or, as Campbell (2008) calls it, a new "home." The actions of a role model—Shingen—guide the hero through his journey.

The thief's transformation brings us back to the idea of the shaman/teacher. In *Kagemusha*, Shingen is the shaman. His social and historical position challenges and reshapes the primary hero's morals. Prince (1991, p. 276) points out that in the case of *Kagemusha*, "[a]s Shingen leaves the room after his first meeting with the thief, the soon-to-be kagemusha (double) bows to the ground, but the lord has already gone. The thief bows before an empty presence, and Kurosawa ends the sequence with this image, thus establishing the basic metaphor of the film, the tenacity with which Shingen's influence continues to shape the clan's fortunes even after his absence." Thus, Shingen's death does not mean the demise of his political ideology, as the double progressively merges with the politics of the lord and the clan. Once on the battlefield, he is in charge of his community.

The conclusion of the film offers a tragic ending for the Takeda clan. Prince (1991, p. 276) argues that at the end of *Kagemusha*, "[i]nstead of showing the emergence of a nation, Kurosawa offers a vision of failure, the doom of the Takeda clan. Instead of the constructions of durable political institutions that would last for centuries, he gives us the rivers of blood and the piles of dead." This is an accurate reading, though somewhat unsatisfactory once we study it based on the theme of death in parallel with political events in 16th-century Japan. It is true that on the screen, viewers witness death, blood, and annihilation. Nevertheless, the death of the Takeda clan means the survival of a larger community. Therefore, Shingen's attitude toward war, death, and history is proven correct. It has worked for the benefit of other clans, as they have won the war.

In Leone's cinematic texts, a large-scale battle carries a different ide-

Part Two—The Hero's Position and the Theme of Death in Battle

ological meaning for the hero than it does in Ford's and Kurosawa's films. To start with, instead of being an enterprise that the hero gets involved with throughout the narrative or as part of the film's conclusion, the battle is a danger zone that the hero should avoid at any cost. Leone's heroes are often too self-centered or caught up in their personal agendas to be concerned with other matters. As the result of such an attitude, the external conflict is often raised due to the actions of the characters motivated by gaining a financial windfall. Such motivation ultimately leads Leone's hero to face the villain in a duel as part of the film's conclusion. The question here is how Leone's hero would respond to the threat of death raised by American Civil War as a form of external conflict. The Civil War not only abolished slavery but, similar to Japan's internal wars, also resolved the regional (at least in terms of a political settlement) and territorial disputes in America. Classic Western films are often concerned with the birth of the American nation. Leone, however, does not refer to this ideological and political transformation aspect of American history in his films.

European Western films (including those directed by Leone) portray their director's interpretation of the Western film's mythopoeia rather than the historical west. Since the European directors were making Western films during the 1960s, culturally and geographically they were not in the genre's heartland. In the 1960s and 1970s, the Western as a filmmaking tradition was past its prime in Hollywood. Directors like Ford, Mann, and Hawks were either approaching the age of retirement or mainly concerned with other genres. In one of his interviews with Frayling (2008), Leone argued that his films were a "myth" about the myth of American Western films. Thus, it is no surprise that a European director like Leone treats the components of the classic Western genre differently from someone like Ford. He does not acknowledge the positive outcome of the Civil War for the nation and its future generations. Leone said in another interview with Frayling (2000, p. 204) that during the making of *The Good, the Bad and the Ugly* "what interested me was, on the one hand, to demystify the adjectives, on the other to show the absurdity of war.... The Civil War which the characters encounter, in my frame of reference, is useless, stupid: it does not involve a 'good cause.'" Leone does not offer a further explanation for why he envisions the Civil War as useless. However, Kitses' (2004, p. 269) ideas can shed further light on this matter: "Leone has said that the Civil War did not involve 'good cause'; slavery's subjects might have insisted on a different perspective, but not a single black face is in evidence. Dramatizing the Civil War at such length and dismissing it as a site of wasted lives,

6. Death, External Conflict and Battle

as Blondie does, without addressing its politics, is a controversial approach perhaps available only to a foreign director." The part of Kitses' writing that can further my theory on death in the battlefield is the idea of "wasted lives."

So far, I have written that in the films of Ford and Kurosawa, the hero's death or survival of the threat of death on the battlefield results in (a) the hero's emotional maturity, (b) his return to some of his generic obligations, and (c) rationalizing the idea that the inner-group conflict is resolved and, subsequently, a nation and its future are forged. Regarding death and its function during the external conflict, Leone's films offer only the first scenario. The hero, after facing the threat of death and surviving it, ponders the absurdity of the war. This new faculty of the hero results in the renewed emphasis of his earlier goal—to escape his surroundings by seeking a fortune. Leone does not suggest any positive outcome for the American Civil War. As a result, he goes against the dominant interpretation of historical events. In other words, Leone reconceptualizes the political struggle in terms of nihilism.

Although Leone does not engage with the Civil War, he returns to some of the classic codes of the Western genre about the advancement of society. To elaborate on this point, I will consider the case of Leone's *Once Upon a Time in the West*. In this film, death, beyond its tragic consequences, is a force that shifts the course of history. It is the initial foundation of a new civilization. Therefore, in this context, death and violence are celebrated as necessary for modernizing society. Leone's approach to death and modernity regarding the position of the heroes and villains means that, by engaging in acts of violence, they contribute to the civilizing process of society. Therefore, if Ford's and Kurosawa's approaches to the birth of a unified nation depend on wars between armies, Leone emphasizes the need for battles among individuals if a society seeks industrial progress. Kitses (2004, p. 270) notes on this matter, "With *Once Upon a Time in the West*, he [Leone] was embracing Ford's central subject of the coming of civilisation, but the mordant Leone inevitably installs death as the foundation upon which the new America rises, the subtext that gives this extraordinary film its unique character." Early in the film, there is a visual indication of this argument when Frank (Henry Fonda), a gunman, massacres the entire McBain family to help Morton, a railroad tycoon, proceed with his business plans for expanding the railroad. Here Leone reviews the Fordian legacy cynically, as innocent people die violently for the modern America to born. As Frank aims to kill McBain's young son, the camera zooms in on his

Part Two—The Hero's Position and the Theme of Death in Battle

weapon, which is the symbol of violence. The gun fires, and the image is juxtaposed with that of an upcoming train from the east—the symbol of modernity and advancement to a nearby town.

Even though violence is a significant aspect of action-packed films, there is a subtle difference in the way that Ford and Leone represent this concept. In Ford's version of the west, violence is only championed if it supports law and order. This idea means that lawmen and gunmen must become allied to challenge the immorality and socially disruptive power of corrupt individuals such as Liberty Valance in *The Man Who Shot Liberty Valance*. In contrast, the law does not have a significant presence in Leone's films. It should also be noted that law in his films is always overwhelmed by the actions of bounty hunters and villains—for example, all the criminals are killed or arrested by freelance gunmen rather than sheriffs. That is why the lawmen have minimal effect on the narrative's progress for Leone. This ideological impotence of the representatives of the law is another of Leone's strategies to depict the extent of corruption within society. Law, like the family, is an absent value in his mythical west.

Furthermore, in Leone's approach to modernization, law (in contrast to Ford's attitude toward American history and ideology) is not a potentially effective social force. It is the violent actions of heroes such as Harmonica (Charles Bronson) and Cheyenne (Jason Robards), working against the violence of villains such as Frank and Morton, that pushes American society toward a new course. It can be argued that, in *Fort Apache*, Thursday's violent attitude toward the Indians is one of the elements pushing the community forward. However, the difference is that violence in this context is a contributing factor rather than the chief social energy that could establish legal institutions. In contrast to these two directors, when Kurosawa presents his audience with the excessive use of graphic violence, as in films such as *Yojimbo*, he is mourning the lack of law and order in society. At the beginning of *Yojimbo*, a stray dog carrying a human hand walks out of the village. The audience and the hero will never learn whose hand it was. This scene shows that the hero has entered a chaotic town stripped of the rule of law.

Leone's approach to American history challenges the modernization of society in the light of its ideological need for violence that destroys the villains and the non-villains (such as the McBain family) alike. The archetypes in *Once Upon a Time in the West* include a criminal who futilely tries to become a businessman (Frank), the obnoxious railroad baron (Morton), a lone avenger (Harmonica) and a romantic bandit (Cheyenne). The

6. Death, External Conflict and Battle

intriguing point is that Leone's heroes in *Once Upon a Time* are well aware of their pending historical obsolescence. Leone, in his interview with Frayling (2000, p. 254), referred to this point by saying that "the story [of *Once Upon a Time in the West*] was about a birth and a death. Before they even come on to the scene, these stereotypical characters know themselves to be dying in every sense, physically and morally—victims of the new era which was advancing." The only person who appears to survive the upcoming social and political changes is Jill (Claudia Cardinale), a former prostitute from New Orleans. As the new town of Sweetwater is born around the railroad, her journey is complete. From a Southern prostitute, she has become the only woman (for the time being) in the upcoming western town. The significant point is that Jill's survival of the threats of death is followed by her new position as the mother of the west. Leone portrays her prominent role in the new community as she walks around and provides the workers with water, keeping their spirits up.

Jill's final position in the film is an intriguing one, for it brings together the interpretations of Leone and Ford on motherhood and the birth of a nation. I have already argued that in classic Westerns (including Ford's films), one of the generic codes indicates that if a fallen woman does not come between moral couples, she can redeem herself through becoming a nurturing mother who marries the hero. In doing so, she will be involved in a cycle of life. The case of Leone's film is almost the same—at least in principle. Jill (unlike, for example, Dallas in Ford's *Stagecoach*) is not a victim of social conservatism. Regardless, I still see Jill as a character who embodies those aspects of traditional morality related to motherhood in that she functions as a caring surrogate mother for Cheyenne and Harmonica, two men who saved her from Frank. She is involved in the cycle of life not in a biological sense but in a historical sense. She is the mother of the modern west and the person who may remember the old west's fading heroes (such as her two male protectors).

The point to consider is what the upcoming modernity has in store for Leone's characters. Leone, in contrast to Ford, does not show the modern west. Instead, he portrays its roots. Harmonica says that "businessmen like Morton will come" to the west. This statement can indicate that, in Leone's version of the modern west, the law is still not a strong social force. "Businessmen like Morton" who hire gunmen like Frank to advance their plans will have the money and the power. This is another example of Leone's ironic point of view toward the west. A unified society, in his vision, does not mean the end of villains. Instead, it means the dawn of a new force of

Part Two—The Hero's Position and the Theme of Death in Battle

antagonism and corruption, which is the monopoly of capitalism, as opposed to the small-scale businesses that Ford champions. Andrea Gazzaniga (2013, p. 53) argues that in *Once Upon a Time in the West*, "Leone marks the end of the great Western, and thus the birth of the new West, with the arrival of the unstoppable train of capitalism." This economic and social force is too wicked, and perhaps too strong, to be challenged. As a result, the hero leaves the newly built town.

Part Three

Narrative Attitude Toward the Hero's Suicide

7

Suicide and Redemption

On rare occasions—to be precise, twice in Ford's films and once in Leone's Westerns—the leading or supporting hero's journey in the film concludes with his/her redemptive suicide. There is no example of redemptive suicide in Kurosawa's films. For Kurosawa, suicide is a sign of despair; once the hero is surrounded by extreme financial (*Red Beard*), political (*Throne of Blood* and *Ran*) and personal (*Rashomon*) circumstances (and there is no possible way for the hero to overcome his/her difficulties), he commits suicide.

In order to understand the redemptive quality of suicide, we need to remind ourselves of its social aspects. Emile Durkheim, in his seminal text *Suicide* (first published in 1898), revolutionized the theoretical understanding of suicide. Related to the uniqueness of each subject of suicide, Durkheim (1952, p. 277) writes that "[e]ach victim of suicide, gives his act a personal stamp which expresses his temperament, the special conditions in which he is involved, and which, consequently, cannot be explained by the social and general causes of the phenomenon." Durkheim, in his writings, concentrates on an individual's mental, social, and financial circumstances in order to analyze the relationship between the said individual's suicide attempt and his community. Based on this analysis, he suggests four types of suicide: egoistic, altruistic, anomic and fatalistic. Durkheim lists most suicide attempts under the first three categories, offering the idea of fatalistic suicide only briefly in his book's footnote. A. Alvarez, in *The Savage God: A Study of Suicide* (1971, pp. 113–114), offers a precise and lucid summary of these types of suicide: "[Durkheim] insisted that every suicide could be classified scientifically as one of the three genre types—egoistic, altruistic, anomic—and that each type was the product of a specific social situation. Thus, egoistic suicide occurs when the individual is not properly integrated into society but is, instead, thrown on his own resources.... The next opposite of all this is 'altruistic suicide.' It occurs when an individual is so completely absorbed in the group that its goals and identity become

7. Suicide and Redemption

his.... Anomic suicide ... is the result of change in a man's social position so sudden that he is unable to cope with his new situation." I will discuss later in this chapter how each case of suicide in the films of Ford, Kurosawa, and Leone links to Durkheim's theory of anomic suicide.

From an existentialist standpoint, Albert Camus, in *The Myth of Sisyphus* (first published in 1942), criticizes the limitations of studying suicide as merely a social phenomenon. Camus (1975, p. 12), after having conceptualized voluntary death as "one truly serious philosophical problem," writes, "Suicide has never been dealt with except as a social phenomenon. On the contrary, we are concerned here, at the outset, with the relationship between individual thought and suicide." He further postulates that an individual privileged with sound emotions and faculties concerns himself with thoughts of suicide. Camus also argues that a person considers committing suicide when the mainstream community/society rejects him. Colin Wilson, in his book *The Outsider* (1970, p. 15), develops on Camus' writings, arguing that "the man in good health is thinking about other things and doesn't look in the direction where the uncertainty lies. And once the man has seen it, the world can never afterward be quite the same straightforward place." Therefore, an outsider, whether real or fictional, may try to find a way into the collective. If his altruistic approach fails, there is a possibility that he will contemplate suicide. In epic genres, the hero is often an outsider seeking integration within the community. However, in the realm of films, instead of committing suicide because he is not welcome in the community, the hero often fights with the villains who threaten the community's safety. The hero's reaction to his position as an outsider is similar to Camus' ideas, as he suggests that, although an individual concerned with an existentialist way of thinking will consider suicide, the act of suicide is not a rational solution to any personal crisis. Camus (1975, p. 7) declares, "Even if one does not believe in God, suicide is not legitimate ... even within the limits of nihilism it is possible to find the means to proceed beyond nihilism." This thinking leads to his conclusion that the point of life (even for an outsider who has encountered life's ordeals) is to live. This idea, in relation to action genres, means that an individual is elevated to the status of the hero, for he does not give up on life despite facing various ordeals. The hero challenges these personal and social tribulations, whatever they may be.

Campbell (2008) suggests that in myths, one dominant characteristic of the hero is that he sacrifices his safety and faces life-threatening ordeals for the sake of others' well-being. Related to film study, this theory means that heroes such as Ethan in *The Searchers*, the samurai in *Seven Samurai*

Part Three—Narrative Attitude Toward the Hero's Suicide

or the unnamed hero in *A Fistful of Dollars*, while aware of the dangers ahead, undertake an uneven battle against the forces of the antagonist. In doing so, they experience the threat of death. In most cases (including the examples above), the hero is not part of a bigger society. Sometimes his actions result in his integration with the community that he has saved from destruction. However, in many cases, he will not bond with the community. This lack of social integration is mainly due to two reasons. First, the hero functions as the sentinel of social conventions and morals of the community (even if his code of conduct is at times opposed to that of the bigger group). Second, the hero in any genre, and particularly in the action genres, takes risks without accepting any tangible reward, including a settled position within a community—he does what is ideologically approved within the context of each society. However, this does not mean that the hero's risk-taking and voluntary death are in tandem. There is a distinction between the two ideas of "a sacrificing hero" and "the hero who attempts suicide."

My argument follows Durkheim's (1952, p. 44) explanation of the etymology of suicide: "The term *suicide is applied to all cases of death resulting directly or indirectly from a positive or negative act of the victim himself, which he knows will produce this result* [emphasis original]." In so writing, Durkheim suggests two dimensions for voluntary death, which are pivotal in studying this theme in films. First, the act of suicide is a conscious one. In the films of Ford, Kurosawa, and Leone, all suicide victims are aware of what they are about to do—they are not delusional or mentally ill. The other point is that in the films of Ford and Leone, those primary or supporting heroes who have a moral or emotionally troubled past attempt suicide. In this light, their suicide, contrary to orthodox Christian doctrine, is a signifier for their redemption. This chapter will answer: (a) how suicide is a final sign of a character's redemption from his past life; (b) how the redemptive potential of death justifies the act of suicide; and (c) what meanings this kind of suicide creates for the two subthemes of death—namely, the cycle of life and the cult of death.

Furthermore, the hero's death due to suicide, in addition to its redemptive quality, can create meaning similar to dying on the battlefield. The hero's passing in these contexts reinvigorates the film's ideologically approved morality for the participants of the hero's cult of death. This point, combined with the action ethos of Western and period drama films, means that the hero's involvement in a battle that contributes to the future safety of society emphasizes the moral codes that a genre film projects. Suicide in the films of Ford, Kurosawa, and Leone metaphorically conveys this read-

7. Suicide and Redemption

ing that a bedroom, a desert, a small house and so on have the potential to be as important as the battlefield (ideologically speaking). The hero's death due to suicide in these locations is identical to his death on a battlefield; if it is justified by the ideological perspective of the film, it can encode its own distinctive social and moral hypothesis.

As I pointed out in Parts One and Two regarding Western and samurai films, similar to ancient warrior cultures, fighting the battle and dying with honor on the battlefield is one of the main concerns of the heroes. Traditionally, death in battle has clarified the social and political implications of these films. Although there are not many examples of suicide in Western films and Kurosawa's works, suicide in these films has its own set of meanings.

From an ideological point of view on Hollywood films, if suicide equals giving up hope, it could not integrate fully into the classic genre's ideology for America, which is contextualized as the land of opportunity and hope. Self-destruction—most notably in the case of primary heroes rather than supporting heroes—is too pessimistic for an American hero. Related to Ford's attitude toward suicide, as McBride (2003) mentions, Ford was brought up as a Catholic. Considering that suicide is stigmatized in the Catholic faith, this is perhaps another reason why Ford engages with the theme of suicide only under specific circumstances.

The limited number of suicides in European Western films in general, and in Leone's films in particular, is due to the following reasons. First, as Frayling (2000) points out, one of the elements that affects Leone's attitude toward suicide, as with Ford, is the Catholic religion; suicide does not have a dignified position according to Catholic teachings. Second, as Leone pointed out in an interview with Frayling (2000), his Western films, as part of the European Western tradition, are a myth about a genre that deals with modern American mythology, ideology, politics, and history. I will demonstrate that Leone follows most of the themes of the classic Western genre, including those that relate to suicide. Third, Leone's characters are often motivated by financial gain. Their fortune-seeking nature makes them too obsessed with personal gain to be concerned with acts of self-destruction. Furthermore, these characters often direct their violent assertiveness toward others. For example, in *The Good, the Bad and the Ugly*, Tuco harasses an old shopkeeper who has done nothing to deserve the abusive treatment. There are only two suicides in Leone's Westerns, found in *For a Few Dollars More* and *A Fistful of Dynamite*.

One of the general principles of Durkheim's philosophy on anomic

Part Three—Narrative Attitude Toward the Hero's Suicide

suicide can be correlated, with extreme care and caution, to the idea of redemptive suicide in the case of the hero with a troubled past in the films that are the concern of this chapter. As noted earlier, Durkheim argues that anomic suicide means that an individual commits suicide when his/her position within a community/group/society suddenly changes. Once a person cannot cope with his/her new position, physically and emotionally, he/she commits suicide. This scenario differs from suicide in a film where the hero is positioned in a situation (e.g., experiencing severe injury) in which suicide is the only way out. The key phrase in Durkheim's writing is the term "sudden change." Similar to most action films, Ford and Leone illustrate a situation in which an individual's circumstances change so radically that he/she is unable to rectify them. In this context, suicide can be the only solution that allows the hero/heroine to keep his/her status while contributing to others' welfare. In parallel, the hero also ends his physical suffering. For example, in the case of Ford's *3 Godfathers*, Pedro's attempt to save a child from death is part of his redemption from his past misdeeds as a bandit. Following his injury due to an accident, Pedro, by killing himself, lets Bob take the newborn baby out of the desert without wasting any time and energy on him.

I will go as far as to say that in Ford's *3 Godfathers* and *7 Women* and Leone's *A Fistful of Dynamite*, suicide is the privilege of those heroes who have accomplished noble, honorable and ideologically approved righteous deeds; their suicide contributes to the cycle of life. Moreover, they have left a cult of death behind that will remember the extent of their heroism as well as their tragic demise. This cult is mainly absent from Kurosawa's films. If it exists, as in the case of *Red Beard*, it will be focused on a character's death/attempt to die. Then it is more of a cult of mourners than a cult of death. The difference between these two concepts is that a cult of death not only mourns but also remembers/creates positive outcomes from the deceased's actions during his/her lifetime.

Those films of Ford and Leone that are concerned with redemptive suicide establish the redemptive ethos of the hero's suicide either visually or verbally. This point means that there are signs in the plot that suggest a character's suicide to be a plausible and heroic act rather than a human tragedy (as indicated by Kurosawa). I will clarify these suggestions below.

In *3 Godfathers*, Ford portrays the risks that the three bandits—Robert "Bob" Hightower (John Wayne), Pedro (Pedro Armendáriz) and William Kennedy "The Abilene Kid" (Harry Carrey, Jr.)—undertake to help a pregnant woman they find in the desert. She dies shortly after giving birth to a

7. Suicide and Redemption

baby boy. The bandits' status is subsequently elevated to that of the infant's godfathers/guardians, as they decide to save him from the desert. William Darby (2006, p. 4) suggests that one of the concerns of the film is as follows: "*Three Godfathers* (1948) ... utilize[s] the journey motif to show [that its] characters travel within themselves, as well as within the surrounding environments, in order to return to society." During this journey, the Abilene Kid dies of thirst and exhaustion, and Pedro, following a severe injury, commits suicide. In this light, suicide is part of Pedro's personal evolution. Pedro's status as a bandit begins to change as he contributes to the survival of the infant. The sudden change in his health is too harsh; he cannot overcome his life-threatening injuries. It appears that suicide is Pedro's only available way out of physical pain.

Ford hints at the idea of upcoming change in this film when he shows the arrival of the three bandits at a small pool of water. Their images are reflected in the water. Kitses (2004, p. 74) writes on this scene, "Stopping at a pool's edge to water horses and fill canteens prior to their attempt [to rob] the bank, the three principals are reflected upside down, the shot hinting at their distorted values." I suggest that this concept of "distortion," in relation to the future events of this film, can mean that the three bandits belong to the same stock of Ford heroes such as Dallas, Hatfield, Doc Holliday and Colonel Thursday. They may have their share of moral failures, but they do the right and moral deed if the generic circumstances require it.

The proof of the above suggestion in the case of 3 *Godfathers* is that gradually the three bandits depart from their past criminal actions. Losing their personal effects emphasizes the point that these men are being separated from their former lives. Darby (2006, p. 218) specifically highlights this point: "A ... symbolic pattern centers on the physical losses the three godfathers experience as they travel through the desert. Their disposal of saddles, bedrolls, and other gear, as well as the catastrophic loss of their horses, dramatizes how they must lose their lives in crime to attain better lives on earth or (presumably) in heaven." Once they find the pregnant woman in the middle of the desert, they have a new goal: to save her and her soon-to-be-born child. This goal overtakes their moral distortion. Their honorable purpose leads to the infant's survival of the threat of death, albeit at the expense of the Abilene Kid's death and Pedro's suicide. Their passing is not a mere tragedy, since it has a positive impact on someone else's life and future.

Pedro's suicide is what Hagin (2010) would call the "intermediary death." This event functions as a bridge between the previous events of the

Part Three—Narrative Attitude Toward the Hero's Suicide

film (those that portrayed Pedro as a bandit with a sense of positive morality as he shares his water with a mother and her newborn baby) and the coming events of the narrative. As a result, his death (alongside that of the Abilene Kid, who nurtures the baby by feeding him and singing him to sleep) functions as a strategy to guide the viewers toward a common theme in Ford's texts—namely, that the future of the society is built upon the sacrifices of brave individuals (although these sacrifices may lead to death). Darby (2006, p. 218) points to this very idea: "Pedro (Pedro Armendariz) and the Abilene Kid die to ensure that the future may live—a seemingly natural human arrangement to which these lawbreakers acquiesce." Pedro's suicide has effects on the cycle of life similar to that of Hatfield's death in *Stagecoach*. Therefore, the former's death not only establishes his redemption but also indicates that others (such as the baby) will survive the threat of death. Thus, his death reinforces the central ideological perspective of the film.

The connection between Bob's redemption and Pedro's suicide is quite significant. To begin with, Bob is the leader of the three godfathers, a point that is emphasized by casting a star actor (John Wayne) as Bob Hightower. His redemption thus carries more moral weight than the supporting heroes' redemption. At the crucial moment, Pedro asks for Bob's pistol in order to commit suicide. In doing so, Pedro strips Bob of one last attachment to his previous life as a bank robber. I see this pistol as the most morally compromised object in Bob's possession—it is the device that has been used previously against the law-abiding members of society, such as the law officers in the town of Welcome, where the three bandits attempted a bank robbery. Thus Pedro, in killing himself with Bob's pistol, contributes to Bob's redemption. This point emphasizes the moral extent of his suicide, in that it redeems more than one person from an unsavory past. Therefore, although suicide is an unorthodox style of death in most action films, once it shows redemptive quality for one or more characters, it has the capacity to encode positive messages for a film.

On the surface of classic films, once an individual takes his own life, the civilized community does not celebrate his memory. It can be argued that the "return to society," as Darby (2006, p. 218) calls it, is interrupted in this scenario. I disagree with such readings. I argue that, in spirit, a hero who commits suicide can still be integrated into the community. This integration is possible due to the formation of the deceased's cult of death. In *3 Godfathers*, initially, the dying mother chooses to name her son Robert William Pedro Hightower. This cardinal moment projects the meaning that the mother, though unaware of the potential death of her son's godfathers,

7. Suicide and Redemption

positions her infant as Pedro and the Kid's legacy. Later, Pedro and the Kid constantly argue with Bob over saying the baby's name in full. Beyond its light and humorous effects, this argument points out that the three are anticipating that this child will be the person to carry their names into the future. In a related note, I refer to Carl Watkins' book *The Undiscovered Country*, in which he (2013, p. 12) writes about an attitude observed among parents from the medieval era until now: "Medieval men and women hoped to live on, as many modern ones do, in their children." The same can be said about the three guardians of Ford's Western.

The sign of Pedro's and Kid's posthumous entrance into society is the name of the infant: Robert William Pedro Hightower. This situation is similar to the conclusion of *Fort Apache*, as Philadelphia's son carries the names of his two dead grandfathers and the new commander of the fort. In *Fort Apache*, the three officers are part of a generation that transforms the ideological wasteland that is the American frontier to a civilized community. In *3 Godfathers*, the three bandits overcome the spiritual wasteland symbolized by their journey through the blazing waterless desert.

Furthermore, in the case of *3 Godfathers*, the infant's name confirms the redemption of the two bandits who died while trying to save him from the threat of death. I suggest this reading based on a visual sign toward the end of the film: As an exhausted Bob walks in the desert carrying the newborn in his arms, he begins to hallucinate due to exhaustion as he sees the phantasms of Pedro and the Kid encouraging him to keep going. Their ghostly presence, although justifiable due to Bob's thirst and fatigue, suggests that the dead are forgiven for their past conduct as bandits. Moreover, the ghosts of the Abilene Kid and Pedro are divine messengers encouraging Bob not to give up. This function of the ghosts is similar to their function in ancient myths. Levi-Strauss (1978, p. 32) writes on this point, "In mythology ... we have deities or supernaturals, who play the roles of intermediaries between the powers above and humanity below."

Another point that one should not overlook is the significance of the wasteland/desert as the place where two of the redeemed heroes ultimately die. Martin Lefebvre, in *Landscape and Film* (2006, p. 86), writes on the role of the desert in Western films, "The desert is an absolute or pure landscape, with few or no marks of human presence, which magnifies its connotations within the religious imagery." Although Lefebvre applied this theory to study the films of D.W. Griffith (1875–1948), it can also be linked to the locus of suicide in *3 Godfathers*. Pedro's ghost can be seen as that spiritual reference, suggesting that his death in the wasteland of the desert

Part Three—Narrative Attitude Toward the Hero's Suicide

has not been in vain. The presence of his spirit in a happy disposition means that, contrary to Christian orthodoxy, he is not damned to hell for committing suicide.

I note that the redemptive quality of suicide has a further function in that it can be used to show the primary hero's death as part of a film's conclusion. Neupert (1995, p. 32) writes that "[the] ending stands as the final address to the spectator, the place where the story may be resolved and where the narrative discourse may close." Neupert's comment is as cliché as it can possibly be; nevertheless, regarding the theme of suicide, this means that the hero's attempt to end his own life has the ability to establish the final ideological message of the film. This idea is quite significant in the case of classic films. According to Bordwell et al. (1985), a classic hero's actions will lead to clear results within the timeframe of the film. Neupert (1995, p. 38) expands on this idea by arguing that "[t]he emphasis on character action and carefully limited time and space allows the classical cinema, like the realistic novel, to embed itself within a codified diegesis that lends a sort of self-induced and plausible predestination to its actions and events." In this sense, suicide is an indication of a hero's change of character during the film. In addition, as argued earlier, the hero's suicide and his redemption can be a sign that, at the expense of one person's life, the future of other individuals is saved from the threat of destruction. The suicides of Dr. Cartwright (Anne Bancroft) in Ford's *7 Women* and Sean in Leone's *For a Fistful of Dynamite* portray such closure. In both films, the hero's suicide indicates his/her redemption and begets the possibility of a better life for other individuals. However, the quality of this future is different from one filmmaker's vision to another.

7 Women shows the story of a Christian mission in northern China toward the end of the 1930s. Ford (in Peary, 2001, p. 73) identifies this film's genre as a Western by saying that *7 Women* is "a western that takes place in China, and in which all the cowboys are women." In the course of the film, a group of violent bandits captures the missions and its female residents. One of the captives, Dr. Cartwright, contributes to the survival of others by becoming the concubine of Tunga Khan (Mike Mazurki), the chief of the bandits. In doing so, she gains access to her medical case, which enables her to help a pregnant middle-aged woman give birth. Realizing that the child will die if he stays in the mission, Cartwright agrees to remain with Tunga Khan so that the others, including the newborn baby, can leave the mission. As the group of women is freed, and thus saved from the bandits, Cartwright poisons her captor and then commits suicide.

7. Suicide and Redemption

Cartwright's entrance to the mission is reminiscent of Ford's heroes from his previous Western films. (For example, she has the same cowboy attire as John Wayne in most Ford's films.) Although Cartwright is a character who is unable to conform to the norms of the community, she still makes great sacrifices for the sake of the said community.

There are two sides to Cartwright's suicide. First, considering that her sexual conduct is ideologically stigmatized within the context of traditional Christian morality, as she is forced to live as the concubine of a bandit, her death saves her from further moral and sexual humiliation. Also, and closer to my theoretical framework, her suicide, similar to Pedro's, is the final stage of a troubled hero's redemption from past actions. Earlier in the film, we see Cartwright as a leading heroine who drinks, blasphemes, smokes heavily and, above all, admits to maintaining a sexual relationship with a married man back in America. According to the dominant morality of classical Hollywood films, these behaviors are not suitable for a woman.

Concerning Cartwright's actions, I return to my earlier observation that if a female character disrupts the moral and traditional romantic union promoted rigorously by the classic film's synthesis, she will be punished. Wood (2009, p. 593) argues that the importance of a traditional romantic union lies its embodiment of "civilized values." This embodiment guarantees the presence of these values for the future society inside and outside the narrative. If we consider the moral weight of this system, it is understandable that those who disturb this system of morality are punished. Hence, Cartwright shares the same fate as Chihuahua in *My Darling Clementine*. Nevertheless, there are some significant differences between the two characters. Chihuahua's status is that of someone who disturbs a marital union. Also, she does not undertake any heroic action. By contrast, although Dr. Cartwright is an adulteress who comes between a man and his legal wife, she saves a newborn baby and his mother from the threat of death. This scenario shows her integration with some of the classic codes of the Western genre. Kitses' (2004, p. 131) ideas regarding Cartwright's suicide can be linked to my argument: "Ford was working with his usual Western formula of the imperiled community and the heroic, redemptive action that preserves the future." Therefore, it is reasonable to infer that her death has more of a redemptive quality than a mere punishment.

In the realm of classic cinema, only the leading hero's death has the potential to conclude not just his/her life but also the film. War, death and sexual degradation suddenly change Cartwright's life in the mission. This profound and sudden alteration can be seen as the anomic aspect of her

Part Three—Narrative Attitude Toward the Hero's Suicide

suicide. It should also be recalled that she is the primary heroine of a film that, chronologically speaking, was made in an era when the values that classic films promoted had lost their significance. Related to this argument, Wood (in Caughie, 1981, p. 96) writes, "Ford's values [in his 1960s films] are not really reversed; they are ... weakened." Nevertheless, Ford still follows most of the conventions of classic films: Cartwright will be redeemed from her troubled past as she overcomes various ordeals in her journey within the film's story, but she will not survive beyond the end of the film.

In the final act of the narrative, Cartwright undergoes her ultimate test once the newborn baby and the women of the mission are saved from the violent and uncivilized actions of the bandits (killing innocent people, raping women, and so on). The camera depicts her in traditional Chinese garb, holding a lantern and entering the building where she and Tunga Khan reside. Her attire is a sharp contrast to her masculine and Western-style costume from the film's beginning. Her oriental garments show her transforming position in the film's story. A significant part of this transformation has occurred under sexual captivity. Her suicide can thus be seen as an action that enables her to achieve freedom in death. McBride (2003, p. 674), opposing Samuel Fuller's assertion that Cartwright commits suicide because her captor is a savage alien, writes that "the doctor's apparent submission to Tunga Khan is a pragmatic decision, not only allowing her charges to escape but also avoiding, by suicide, what surely would be a brutal sexual bondage offering little hope of survival."

One could argue that suicide in the above framework is a sign of despair, as McBride reads it. There is a visual reference that can support such a reading: Cartwright leaves the illuminated lantern behind and walks in a dark, narrow corridor that leads to the bandits' room, a possible signal that she has given up hope, symbolized by the light of the lantern, and merged with despair emphasized by the darkness. This argument is valid on the surface. However, I posit that in all cases of suicide due to despair (which I will study in the following chapter), the suicide victims do not have any great or heroic achievement. Therefore, the darkness in this scene can merely mean death, as opposed to despair. In addition, Cartwright is an American heroine. Although she has an ambiguous moral position, she has affected the lives of others around her in a positive and ethical sense. The dark corridor, instead of suggesting a bleak ending, to me emphasizes the depth of the dark, uncivilized and corrupt morality of the Chinese bandits. The corridor indeed leads to the hero's place of death. However, Cartwright's suicide can mark her emancipation from such compromised morality.

7. Suicide and Redemption

It is also unconventional that Ford, one of the masters of classic American cinema, would engage with suicide as a sign of despair. This point requires clarification. As I wrote in the introduction to this book, Mackey-Kallis (2001), following the anthropological theories of Joseph Campbell, identifies a variety of quests that a hero might experience in an American film. One of these is the "grail quest," which means the hero is searching for a new home (either a real home or a new mentality) and, in doing so, will face traumas from his/her past life. Cartwright, in accepting the position of a medical doctor in the mission and leaving America, follows the grail. This quest privileges her with the possibility of reconnecting with her moral roots and leads her to the mission and subsequent suicide/redemption. Kitses (2004, p. 131) points out that Cartwright's death "is Ford's last stand, an apt affirmation of the glory in defeat, of faith's brave light against darkness."

The cult of death that Cartwright leaves behind is the sign that her suicide, although tragic, is not due to despair. This cult includes those whom she has saved from the threat of death and potential sexual slavery. The youngest female of the group, whose virginal presence can suggest innocent, purity and thus righteousness in a classical Hollywood sense, says while traveling away from the Christian mission, "I will not forget her [Dr. Cartwright] as long as I live." This line can mean that the speaker serves as the representative of the deceased's cult of death. She, similar to Wyatt Earp and Captain York, announces the final verdict on the hero's position in the film's story—that is, the hero is dead but not forgotten within the diegesis of the film. This is another indication that Cartwright's suicide has contributed to shaping the film's ideology.

The presence of the theme of suicide in *3 Godfathers* and *7 Women* permits no place for ambiguity—the deceased's cult of death and its potential safety is confidently pronounced. Besides, these films depict the contributions of the dead heroes to the future as idealistically positive. Leone's engagement with the theme of suicide in *A Fistful of Dynamite* is somewhat critical to the dead hero's contribution to the future of society, since the hero's cult of death, in contrast to Ford's films, is not a major aspect of the film.

In *A Fistful of Dynamite*, Leone portrays the unlikely friendship between a runaway Irish revolutionary–turned–explosives expert in Mexico (Sean) and a Mexican bandit/peasant (Juan). Their friendship leads the latter to become involved with the revolution in Mexico. However, Sean (played by James Coburn) commits suicide at the end of the film after suffering a severe spinal injury.

Part Three—Narrative Attitude Toward the Hero's Suicide

Leone, in using flashbacks throughout the film, gradually reveals Sean's emotional traumas. He is a committed revolutionary who has killed a friend/brother in arms for the sake of the Irish revolution. The usage of flashbacks to illustrate a hero/villain mindset is standard practice in Leone's films (as seen in *For a Few Dollars More*, *Once Upon a Time in the West* and *Once Upon a Time in America*). These memories are usually a means of keeping the sense of vengeance alive for the hero as he remembers the past. These reminiscences also enable the villain to identify the vengeful hero. In the context of *A Fistful of Dynamite*, the images of the past function as a mental energy that directs Sean to a melancholic and depressed mood. Coburn's wooden and poignant facial expression portrays this sense of glumness profoundly. However, the hero's traumatized character in this film does not register suicide as a despairing act. Similar to other films examined in this chapter, Sean's suicide suggests redemption.

Scholars and writers such as Frayling and Kitses argue (and I agree with them) that in Leone's Westerns, heroes do not change and develop as they do in classic Westerns. Frayling (2008) goes as far as arguing that, prior to *A Fistful of Dynamite*, there was no such thing as "character development" in Leone's films. I further argue that this is the case because Leone positions his heroes in such dire situations that even if they wanted to change, there is not much hope for their social surroundings to do so. These characters, after all, stay put in their emotional mindset, as they do not welcome change. This strategy is perhaps the only available means of guaranteeing their survival. However, this is not the case with Sean and Juan in *A Fistful of Dynamite*.

The evolution of Sean's character involves his redemption and suicide. As he is about to kill himself, one final flashback illustrates the idealized image of Ireland's beautiful countryside. This scene is accompanied by Ennio Morricone's orchestral score, which romanticizes and fetishizes this rich imagery. Kitses (2004, p. 328) writes that "the past for [Sean] is not the site of family dishonor defining him as a revenge hero. Rather, he is driven by guilt, fleeing himself rather than pursuing satisfaction." Beyond killing his friend, Sean feels guilt for having destroyed an idealistic way of life in Ireland. In his reminiscences, Ireland is shown as a bright milieu where young men share everything, including the women they love. Sean's act of recollecting the past at the hour of his death is not so much a memory as a fantasy of a life that could have been. The life he perceives in his hallucinations after being mortally wounded in battle is happy and perfect; yet he is unable to reach it. Regardless, Sean, in his last moments, even in

7. Suicide and Redemption

an imaginary state of mind, returns to his roots in Ireland. This is quite similar to the effects of Hatfield's redeeming death in *Stagecoach* (explained in Part One).

Sean in *A Fistful of Dynamite* has contributed to the cycle of life in an ideological sense. He has battled for the sake of a revolution. However, Leone approaches this idea of the cycle of life differently than, say, Ford would do. For Leone, a hero's involvement with the cycle of life is more abstract than it is for Ford. In *A Fistful of Dynamite*, Sean's suicide does not lead to much social change. Leone offers no visual or verbal signs that would suggest a conventional ending similar to that of Ford's films. Leone (in Frayling, 2000, p. 306) says, "I am a pessimist by nature. With John Ford, people look out of the window with hope. Me, I show people who are scared even to open the door. And if they do, they tend to get a bullet right between the eyes." Sean and Juan are among the rare Leone heroes who change over the course of the film. This change offers a glimmer of hope, which is the thematic ground in which Leone and Kurosawa's films come closer together as situations change. The impact of this change in Leone's film stands in stark contrast to Ford's take on the hero's death, as Ford offers visual and verbal guarantees that the hero's hardships will bring about a prosperous life for the majority.

The ambivalent nature of the cult of death in Leone's films also contrasts with Ford's approach to the same concept. At the end of *A Fistful of Dynamite*, Juan is the sole representative of Sean's cult of death. It can be said that the future generations do not function as his cult of death; if Sean had a traditional collective cult of death (as the fallen heroes do in Ford's films), there would be signs and references to that end, whereas in *A Fistful of Dynamite* there are none. In Leone's films, unlike Ford's, those who survive the threat of death do not evolve to become characters that respect and promote conventional moralities. Juan is such a character. There is no indication that he will not return to stealing and raping once the film is over. Frayling (2000, p. 326) points out that "in the final exchange between Sean and Juan, as the Irishman lies dying, Juan says, 'You leave me now and what's going to happen to me, huh?' 'They'll make you general,' replies Sean. 'I DON'T WANT TO BE NO GENERAL,' comes the retort." This line is the crucial piece of dialogue establishing Juan's final position in the film—namely, Juan is safe from the threat of death and has become a symbol of the revolution. However, Juan's fate in the film does not mean a conventional ending for him. His family and his only friend are all killed. He also is not that happy about being promoted to general. In short, he does not respond

Part Three—Narrative Attitude Toward the Hero's Suicide

to his change of social position as a classic hero would. His character is positioned in an ambiguous situation, for at the moment of transition his equilibrium remains intact.

Furthermore, Juan has not become a revolutionary of his own accord. The bank robbery scene explains this idea. Here Juan believes that he is about to undertake the biggest heist of his career. Once inside the bank, however, he finds out that the vaults are filled with political prisoners. In freeing them, he will be announced as the "great hero of the revolution." In short, he is situated in unfamiliar social and political territory. Juan's moral and generic ambivalence toward his new position becomes his defining characteristic. That is why at the conclusion of the film, unlike the Fordian hero, he does not have an accommodating approach as the dead hero's representative of his cult of death. There is one line in the film that pronounces his character's ambiguity: "What about me?" This is the last line in the film; it suggests that the hero's main concern is not the well-being of a community/society. Rather, he is afraid of being lonely now that his only friend has committed suicide. After all, similar to Leone's other heroes, Juan is a narcissist. In relation to the theme of death, this can mean that society does not yet recognize the surviving hero as a participant in a cult of death. As I argued in Part One, a member of a deceased's cult of death is usually living according to the conventional values in society, which certainly does not apply to Juan.

8

Suicide and Despair

There are examples of suicide due to despair in the films of Kurosawa and Leone, but this type of voluntary death is absent from Ford's films. While this discrepancy may be primarily due to censorship codes that were imposed on Hollywood films during Ford's time, this type of suicide nevertheless has no place in Ford's ideology. I have previously explained the ideological and generic *raison d'être* for the absence of despairing suicide in Ford's films. Hereafter, I will consider the following hypothesis: in the films of Kurosawa and Leone, suicide due to despair depicts an individual's response to the emotionally or financially troubled environment/society in which that individual resides.

I have offered this premise based on Prince's ideas (1991, p. 243) regarding the effects of the works of the Russian novelist Fyodor Dostoevsky (1821–1881) on Kurosawa's films: "Like Dostoevsky, Kurosawa has always been an artist of the apocalypse. Like Dostoevsky's, Kurosawa's characters always hover on the brink of spiritual catastrophe, of a trial that will test them to their utmost, take them through fires that will either consume or purify." Although Dostoevsky and Kurosawa worked in different media, historical backgrounds and times, they were concerned with the ways that financial and psychological pressures can lead to an individual's depression. Feeling despair can motivate the individual toward murder or suicide.

It should not go unsaid that suicide as a ritualistic tradition, in contrast to western social attitudes, is a significant aspect of samurai culture. In Japan, *seppuku* or *hara-kiri* (that is, the act of cutting one's belly open with a dagger or short sword and disemboweling oneself) dates to almost a millennium ago. *Seppuku* has experienced its own historical and social evolution and morphed into other varieties. Andrew Rankin, in *Seppuku: A History of Samurai Suicide* (2011, p. 10), writes, "Seppuku can be spontaneous or premeditated, voluntary or obligatory, public or private. It can be a solemn ceremony or dramatic theatre … when it is no longer possible to live proudly, the samurai should endeavor to die proudly, and the proudest

Part Three—Narrative Attitude Toward the Hero's Suicide

samurai death is seppuku." Suicide as a way of saving one's face/personal dignity in the event of failing to achieve one's goals is an important theme in Japanese culture. Mamoru Iga, in *The Thorn in the Chrysanthemum* (1986, p. 139), notes, "The major characteristics of Japanese culture—monism, groupism, authoritarian familism, and accommodationism—contribute much toward producing a wide goal-means [sic] discrepancy, leading to the feeling that 'there is no other way out.'" This feeling of hopelessness means that the act of suicide is not the privilege of warriors; each individual, regardless of his/her social class, can commit suicide. As discussed in the introduction to this book, a Japanese sage, Miyamoto Musashi, suggests that dying for a moral reason within Japanese cultural norms is available to all social classes. However, this method of death does not have a pronounced presence in Kurosawa's films. In previous sections, I have written extensively on Kurosawa's humanist and somewhat democratized approach to life and death. In his films, he promotes the idea of living and doing the right deed rather than giving up hope and killing oneself. In all of his *jidaigeki* films, there are only four that feature cases of suicide (*Rashomon, Throne of Blood* [adapted from Shakespeare's *Macbeth*], *Red Beard* and *Ran* [adapted from Shakespeare's *King Lear*]).

I also argued in the introduction that Leone, similar to philosophers such as Nietzsche, is concerned with the idea of a world in chaos: the law officers lack approved traditional morality, the representation of violence is omnipresent throughout all his Westerns, there is no sense of real community in his films, and so forth. Moreover, Leone's money-obsessed heroes are not usually privileged with spiritual/moral redemption at the end of the film. In most cases, their main achievement will be having acquired some wealth by the film's conclusion. The point here is that Leone's heroes are indifferent to society's moral crisis. Their reaction contrasts with that of Kurosawa's heroes since these protagonists respond to the social chaos as they selflessly take action against it.

To understand the various characteristics of despairing suicide, I will study Kurosawa's *Red Beard* and Leone's *For a Few Dollars More*. There can be some concerns regarding the objective behind analyzing the former film with regard to the theme of suicide. The two main genres in the Japanese film industry are *jidaigeki* and *gendaigeki*. Richie (2005, p. 23) writes that the former category "now defines all period films," while the latter genre is concerned with stories that occur after 1868 (i.e., the end of the Tokugawa period and the beginning of the Meiji Restoration). Since the story of *Red Beard* takes place during the Tokugawa bakufu, it is a *jidaigeki* film. There

8. Suicide and Despair

are two further points to make. First, *Red Beard* is not the only Kurosawa film that shows an awareness of the themes of suicide and despair. However, since this film's plot narrates three accounts of such suicide with various moral and generic implications, it is a compelling opportunity to study the meanings that despairing suicide creates for his films. Second, although *Red Beard* is not an action period film, it exemplifies most of Kurosawa's concerns about the value of life, personal sense of honor, and group dynamics that are addressed in his *jidaigeki* films.

Red Beard narrates the arrival of Noboru Yasumoto (Yuzo Kayama), a recently graduated doctor from Nagasaki, at a publicly funded clinic in a small town of Koishikawa in the late Tokugawa period. Yasumoto's pride in his modern education and abilities as a doctor put him in conflict with the head of the clinic, Dr. Kyojo Niide (Toshiro Mifune), nicknamed Red Beard. Throughout the film, Yasumoto, in observing other individuals' encounters with death or the threat of death, learns valuable lessons about his limitations as a human being and a doctor. By the film's conclusion, he has evolved into a humble, humane hero, typical of Kurosawa's films. Like the ronin in *Sanjuro*, Watanabe in *Ikiru* and others, Yasumoto learns that the point of one's existence is to help others and contribute to improving their dire living conditions. Through bringing about others' happiness, an individual can find psychological and spiritual solace.

In *Red Beard*, Kurosawa covers a variety of subplots, including three suicides. Prince (1991, p. 236) writes that "[w]here the narrative of *Seven Samurai* ... was oriented by and developed toward a single goal—defeat of the bandits—and featured the kind of tight narrative construction typical of Hollywood productions, *Red Beard* moves in many directions simultaneously as it explores the lives of the clinic patients and their past and present suffering." Each of the subplots in *Red Beard* has elements that can be interpreted as despair. The first case relates the voluntary death of a young woman, Onaka (Miyuki Kuwano), who left her husband, Sahachi (Tsutomu Yamazaki). Her husband, who is terminally ill, recalls the account of this suicide. (The effects of his death due to illness will be covered in Part Four.) Prince (1991, pp. 240–241) summarizes the roots of Onaka's suicide as follows: "Sahachi relates [a] long narrative that has emotional misery at its core. He married a woman promised to another man. Feeling ashamed and sinful over breaking the other engagement, she kills herself. Believing that he caused her suffering and that of the other man as well, Sahachi buries her next to the clinic and devotes his life to working for others." I would add to this description that Onaka's despair is not limited to

Part Three—Narrative Attitude Toward the Hero's Suicide

the breaking of her marriage promise. Through the dialogue, Kurosawa portrays her as an emotionally troubled individual. For example, she says that one of the reasons she ended her relationship with Sahachi is that this relationship "was too happy." She also argues that she did not deserve that happiness, for she had broken up with her fiancé in order to marry Sahachi. Later, after leaving the latter, once she learns about the damage that her absence has caused to his physical and emotional health, she commits suicide.

Some readers may argue that Onaka's suicide can be seen as redemption for her past conduct. I do not read it as such. In the previous chapter I wrote that redemptive suicide involves a heroic act—that is, it occurs as an individual is saving another person from the threat of death or contributing to others' survival or the forging of a cycle of life. Onaka's suicide does not have such impacts. Suicide due to despair destroys an existing family or disrupts the inception of a potential cycle of life. In *Red Beard*, Onaka has a young son from her second marriage. Her maternal abilities are visually shown on screen as she feeds the child. In killing herself, she robs the toddler of a nurturing and caring mother. She disturbs the function and balance of a cycle of life. This result is similar to what happens to some of Ford's characters. For example, in *My Darling Clementine*, Chihuahua interrupts the relationship between Holliday and Clementine, so that there is no potential cycle of life available to them. In *Red Beard*, Onaka's cycle of life is severely damaged. The difference is that Chihuahua's death is a punishment for destroying the cycle, whereas Onaka's death damages an existing family.

The lack of personal redemption for a film character does not mean that this individual lacks a sense of honor. I refer to the teachings of Musashi, who (cited in Tsunetomo, 2008, p. 23) writes that "in the way of dying there is no distinction between samurai, Buddhist priests, women and the lower classes from the peasants on down." In *Red Beard* Onaka kills herself because she can no longer live with her past conduct.

Furthermore, suicide due to despair affects the cult of death in a way that is opposite to the effects of a redemptive suicide. Redemptive suicide, as stated before, can mean a definite ending for the cult members (Ford's approach to the concept), wherein the majority of all the questions raised by the narrative are answered. However, in some cases, it can also mean an ambiguous position for the cult members in the film's conclusion (Leone's take on the subject), where the moral and social future of those saved from the threat of death is not clear. In both scenarios, the lives of the cult mem-

8. Suicide and Despair

bers are protected from the threat of death due to the actions of the departed individual. The theme of suicide due to despair does not project the same result since it does not involve a heroic deed.

There is also a similarity between the two themes of voluntary death in relation to the cult of death. Both types of suicide can challenge the morals of the potential participants of a deceased's cult of death. This challenge has an educational quality in that it motivates the main and supporting heroes to be better human beings. In *Red Beard*, two members of Onaka's cult of death experience the above challenge, which subsequently alters their position in the film's plot. Her act of self-destruction, despite not coming from heroic actions and therefore not leading to her redemption, functions as contributing factor in Sahachi's moral transformation, for it teaches him about his responsibility to others. He evolves from a depressed individual into the involved hero that Kurosawa champions in his oeuvre. This point means that Sahachi devotes the rest of his life to helping others. That is why, even during his illness, he works hard to buy food for the impoverished residents of the clinic. In witnessing his ex-wife's suicide, Sahachi begins to make sacrifices for the sake of others. His sacrificial behavior is his salvation from the traumas of the past. This reading is in parallel with Richie's (1996, p. 172) writings: "In the first account of suicide ... [Onaka's] death convinces Yamazaki [Sahachi] that it is only by living for others that one can live at all." A Kurosawa hero usually puts others' needs ahead of his own. In doing so, he gains wisdom. The sign of this result in *Red Beard* is that early in the film most of the characters complain about the plain clothing of the patients in the clinic. It is Sahachi who points out that the simple clothes will show dirt easily, so the doctors can keep the invalids clean. Sahachi's newfound understanding of the surrounding environment, which is derived from his commitment to others, is one of the legacies of Onaka's suicide.

This legacy indirectly affects the faculty of Yasumoto as well. Up until the moment when he hears about Onaka's suicide and its considerable influence on Sahachi's life, he refuses to change his upper-class garments to the simple attire of the clinic's medical staff. Mellen (1976, p. 53) writes about the general attitude of this film, which can also be related to the evolution of Yasumoto's character: "From *Red Beard* on, he [Kurosawa] turns to basic and simple human frailties, dedication to helping people." In relation to the theme of suicide in *Red Beard*, I see this message as an emphasis on the profound sense of morality raised by despairing suicide in participants of a departed character's cult of death. Following Sahachi's passing, Yasumoto's

Part Three—Narrative Attitude Toward the Hero's Suicide

character is transformed, as he changes his clothes and begins to work officially under the guidance of Dr. Niide. This attitude of the cult of death in Kurosawa's film is somewhat similar to what is seen in Ford's films. In *Fort Apache*, following Thursday's death, Captain York takes over the command of the fort; he changes his attire and puts on a proper army uniform, as Thursday would do. Moreover, York's political concerns and his conduct toward the Indians become more like Thursday's. In short, Thursday's death has contributed to the evolution of York's character.

This transformation of a character emphasized through the change of clothes is a strategy observed in the works of Ford and Kurosawa. The difference between the work of these two filmmakers regarding the theme of suicide is that the redemptive suicide (in Ford's films) functions as a moral trigger for the cult members; as a result, they undertake actions that are similar to those of the deceased. These efforts also (in Kurosawa's films) compensate for the failings of the deceased, since the individual who commits suicide due to despair has not performed a heroic act and, therefore, is not redeemed from his former actions. According to this argument, it can be said that one of the core meanings of suicide due to despair is that it shows the value of life and living morally according to one's social norms and conventions in order to compensate for one's past mistakes. In this sense, an individual's suicide evolves from its controversial nature to function as a drive that can motivate others to lead a morally approved life.

The second attempt at suicide in *Red Beard* is committed by an unknown young female patient solely referred to as Mantis (Kyoko Kagawa), an emotionally unbalanced individual who murders her lovers after sexual intercourse. She is confined in a room separate from the clinic's main building, away from the rest of the patients. Although her solitary residential arrangement is a medical necessity, it also establishes her position as an outsider who is kept away from the community. Niide interprets her suicide attempt as a sign that her emotional health is improving, meaning that she can now understand the depth of her earlier crimes. Furthermore, unlike Onaka's suicide, Mantis' suicide attempt is not shown; the audience learns about it through dialogue. There are two recognizable reasons for this: First, the visual representation of Onaka's suicide highlights its significance regarding the educational quality of despairing suicide (as noted earlier). Second, it shows what Sahachi has seen first-hand that has motivated him to live as a selfless human being.

Throughout this book, I have written extensively on the idea that most heroes in a variety of cinematic traditions lack an altruistic attitude. Mantis,

8. Suicide and Despair

though an outsider, is not the kind of hero who seeks integration within the community. There are no visual or verbal references suggesting otherwise. Likewise, since her suicide attempt fails, there is no function and reason for creating a cult of death. The absence of a cult, however, does not mean the lack of moral education. Niide's speech about Mantis' feelings of abandonment and suicide has the same educational quality that her cult of death would have had. Kurosawa's humanistic approach demonstrates that even an individual as tormented and emotionally distorted as Mantis deserves love, respect, and empathy.

Through Mantis' suicide attempt, Kurosawa illustrates her effort to challenge her situation, which can subsequently change her position within the film's story. Wilson (1970, p. 116) writes, "The Outsider wants freedom. He [she in the case of Mantis] does not consider that the ordinary once-born human being *is* free. The fact remains that the Outsider *is* a rarity among human beings—which places him [or her] rather in the position of the soldier who claims he is the only one step in the platoon." This argument explains Mantis' role in the film. She attempts suicide, for, as Niide says, "she cannot face what she has done in the past." In short, she cannot accept herself and strives for emancipation from her past.

Lessons learned from an individual's suicide due to despair revive the sense of social concern within the other film characters. In *Red Beard*, the lessons learned from Onaka's and Mantis' suicides are on display in the case of the last suicide in the film, in which all the members of a low-income family have taken rat poison. All of the doctors and kitchen maids in the clinic do their best to revive them. Out of the family of five, two of the children die; the parents and their youngest son, Chobo (a young thief), survive. Prince (1991, p. 246) writes that, after escaping death after taking the poison, Chobo "radically proposes an ultimate power to the force for good. It completes the logic of the film as a whole, which demonstrates not just the annulment of time but the creation of a positive karma, in which the inevitably of suffering is repeated." It can be said that Chobo, as a child, is not fully responsible for his suicide attempt. However, Kurosawa, through dialogue, suggests otherwise, for Chobo says that "we decided it was best" to kill ourselves ("we" in this case refers to his family). The collective group, under so much financial pressure and shame because of Chobo's thievery, decide to die. This suicide is quite significant regarding the film's attitude toward the theme of death, for it occurs in the last quarter of the narrative, giving a feeling of closure not only to the story but also to the ideological stand of the film in regard to social problems such as poverty. It also shows

Part Three—Narrative Attitude Toward the Hero's Suicide

the depth of the humane side of some of the film's characters that Kurosawa has shown us up to this point—for example, the kitchen maids, who earlier in the film chased Chobo because he had stolen rice from them, are the ones who pray for his survival. This kind of prayer for the dead or dying dates to the Tokugawa era. As part of the rituals for the invalid, the family members/friends would call the name of the individual whom they wanted to revive (e.g., Chobo in *Red Beard*). This tradition, according to Hur (2007, p. 142), is called "bringing back to life (sosei)." Moreover, the custom of calling the name to a well, as seen in *Red Beard*, is common in northern Musashi and western Tsugaru areas in Japan.

Chobo's survival emphasizes once again Kurosawa's assumption, represented in his *jidaigeki* and *gendaigeki* films, that living as moral and decent human beings is one of the main points of life. Yoshimoto (2000, p. 332) argues that those film scholars and critics who are supportive of this film read it as "the celebration of, and the ultimate faith in, human compassion, goodness, and altruism." Financial hardships should not prevent individuals from achieving this morality. They are ordeals that an individual should try to overcome in the life journey in order to reach a mature state of mind or (as Campbell and Mackey-Kallis suggested) a new home.

As part of this film's conclusion, Yasumoto, who is heartbroken in the beginning due to a failed romance, finally overcomes his depression and marries another woman. Although the hero does not marry because of romantic love, this conclusion shares similarities with the happy endings of many classic Hollywood films, including most of Ford's films. In addition, Yasumoto declines the offer to become the shogun's private doctor, which was his initial professional goal. He has decided to live in the impoverished environment of the hospital with his new bride and continue helping the poor patients. In short, from a medical doctor who is inconsiderate of others' needs and well-being, he has transformed into a moral and caring human being. So, the hero's position as an outsider is transformed; he is now a member of the community. In this light, it can be said that the sufferings Yasumoto has encountered during the film (including the suicides of Onaka, Mantis, and Chobo and his family) have positive effects on him, inspiring him to appreciate life. Mellen's (1976, pp. 90–91) arguments can be linked to this idea, as she writes, "The flow of Kurosawa's creative imagination dramatizes the felt life of people who make discoveries, who change and live by new values which permit them to be human." Living by new values, in the case of Yasumoto, means that he has a new attitude toward life at the end of the film as he forges his cycle of life. Here is a sign that,

8. Suicide and Despair

as he contributes to other people's lives and saves them from the threat of death, he is also on a journey that can create new life. Additionally, since he has learned moral lessons from the suicides of others, his new attitude can mean that he will achieve a moral life not experienced by those who attempted suicide. This impact of the despairing suicide stands in contrast to redemptive suicide, as the individual who tries it has already moved away from his/her morally troubled past and contributed to the lives of others (e.g., Dr. Cartwright in *7 Women*).

An individual's suicide due to despair can function as a spur to motivate the hero to act against the forces that have caused the deceased character to commit suicide. This scenario is in line with the revenge motif in Western films. Leone epitomizes this theme in *For a Few Dollars More*, which narrates the partnership between two bounty hunters, Monco (Clint Eastwood) and Colonel Douglas Mortimer (Lee Van Cleef). Their goal is to capture/kill a group of bandits led by El Indio. As the narrative progresses, it becomes clear that Mortimer's primary motivation in facing the bandits is not the prize money. Instead, he wants to avenge the death of his sister, who committed suicide after being raped by El Indio.

The suicide in *For a Few Dollars More* merits the following observations. To begin with, the unnamed victim's act of self-destruction has created emotional trauma for her brother as well as El Indio. Frayling (2000, p. 198) points to the latter situation, writing, "The fact that El Indio remembers this particular incident [rape and suicide], amid all the mayhem and butchery of his subsequent career, shows that the trauma goes deep." To analyze the relationship between the aforementioned emotional anxiety and the theme of death, I will point out that Frayling (2000; 2008) suggests that Mortimer's sister was most likely a virgin before the villain raped her. Her white sleeping gown symbolizes her sexual purity and innocence. I accept this idea and add that her initial position in the film is suggestive of the traditional moral codes of the classic Western genre. Moreover, the young woman and her innocence imply that a society can be the locus of morally pure and decent citizens. Her rape and death suggest that these values (and thus the community members) are in peril due to the villains' actions. I suggest this point based on the previously stated theoretical context of Kitses' (2004) argument that family and civilization are lost values in Leone's texts. Based on this idea, it can be said that El Indio represents external compromised moralities. Even the name "Indio" is perhaps an homage to the traditional position of Indians as condemned outsiders in classic Western films. By forcing his way into the core of the community,

Part Three—Narrative Attitude Toward the Hero's Suicide

El Indio affects it for the worse. As a result, Leone's presentation of a once civilized community is sullied alongside its innocent members. Consequently, it can be said that the magnitude of violence and corruption on display in his films demonstrates the extent of the damage that this loss can inflict.

El Indio's act of raping a virgin establishes his corrupt morality and sadistic approach to creating a cycle of life. After experiencing a great deal of despair following an emotional and sexual violation, even though she has the chance to kill her rapist, the victim commits suicide. This experience leaves El Indio emotionally impotent, as indicated by the fact that he keeps remembering the rape and suicide incident. Kitses (2004, p. 264) writes on this matter, "Providing a Freudian spin, the flashbacks give the narrative psychological depth." The intriguing point is that Leone offers the villain, and thus the audience, flashbacks following any act of violence—for example, El Indio remembers the events of the past after he kills his former friend and his family. Remembering the past in relation to the subject of this book means that murdering others functions as an emotional hook which pulls El Indio's attention back to a vital moment in which he destroyed someone else's potential cycle of life. He is a victim of his previous actions.

If we want to understand Colonel Mortimer's response to his sister's suicide, we should first follow his life story. While gathering information about the colonel, Monco finds out that Mortimer was once a brave, devoted soldier—the sort of upright character that we constantly find in Ford's films. The times have changed, however, and society has no place for individuals such as Mortimer. He has become a bounty hunter; yet his actions stem from moral conviction rather than mercenary motives. Similar to the villain, Mortimer keeps remembering his sister's rape and suicide. However, the effects of her suicide on their mentalities differ. Mortimer tells Monco, "One day something happened and made life very precious." It is safe to assume that this "something" was his sister's suicide. In this scene the script is economical,[1] and, more to the point, it is allusive. Unlike most of Leone's scenes, which involve lengthy dialogues (as is the tradition with other Italian Westerns), here the script illustrates the film's philosophical approach to suicide in a few words: life is too valuable to be wasted.

This attitude is similar to Camus' conclusion in his essay on suicide, for he, too, celebrates the value of life, no matter how harsh an individual's living conditions may be. In addition, the above maxim means that for Leone, similar to Kurosawa, the result of a despairing suicide is a deeper

8. Suicide and Despair

understanding of the real value of life by the character who personifies the deceased's cult of death. This type of suicide creates a moral-orientated goal for the protagonist, which in *For a Few Dollars More* is avenging the passing of an innocent person; although Mortimer is a bounty hunter and takes action against the villain, he asks for no financial prize. As part of the film's conclusion, he kills El Indio in a duel. In doing so, he contributes to the betterment of society. Furthermore, Leone's film, unlike most of Ford's films, does not conclude in an idealistic manner. Similar to most of Kurosawa's films, Leone's *For a Few Dollars More* ends with a small glimmer of hope, which proposes that it is possible for a few individuals, or even one, to challenge social problems.

Part Four

The Hero's Natural Death: Narrating the Past and the Way of the Future

9

Natural Death in Ford's Narrative

From the viewpoint of various anthropologists and historians—among others, Philippe Aries, Norbert Elias, and Geoffrey Gorer—since late 19th century there has been a significant evolution of social attitudes toward natural death/death due to illness or old age throughout the world. Death has gone from being a social event to an isolated experience. Aries (1976, p. 12) notes regarding the former attitude in European societies of medieval times, "[Death] was ... a public ceremony. The dying man's bedchamber became a public place to be entered freely." Elias (1985, pp. 43–44) goes further, comparing the modern social attitude toward death to that of sex in the Victorian social dynamics: "With regard to death, the tendency to isolate and conceal it by turning it into a special area has already decreased since the last century, and has possibly increased.... The defensive attitudes and the embarrassment with which, today, people often react to encounters with dying and death fully bear comparison with the reaction of people to overt encounters with aspects of sexual life in the Victorian age."

Moreover, Elias (1985, p. 67) argues that different cultures share similar thoughts on death. One of these is related to my arguments on the cult of death—namely, the idea that "[d]eath hides no secret.... What survives is what he or she [the departed] has given to other people, what stays in their memory." In the case of Kurosawa's films, including *Red Beard* and *Drunken Angel* (1948), the illness of an individual provides the other characters with an opportunity to learn from his achievements and failures. The general understanding of different scholars is that in oriental and occidental burial cultures, the family/friends of a dying person would surround him to perform his final rites. Although these two ideas are concerned with the mourning culture of bygone ages, a trace of their legacies is present in the films that I study. In the cinematic texts of both Ford and Kurosawa, family and friends gather around the invalid until he is dead. However, one significant difference between mourning rituals of the Middle Ages and films that portray the 19th century is that, in the latter, the living people often

9. Natural Death in Ford's Narrative

do not engage in prayers for the dead/dying person. Instead, they approach the death of a beloved person in a secular manner in that they try to remember the actions of the deceased. The lay nature of mourning in these films can be attributed to their status as products of 20th-century artists who were mainly working in secularized contexts. As I will explain later, in these films the mourners try to know the deceased, his morality and his actions in more depth, which contributes to the moral evolution of the bereaved.

My primary goal in studying the natural death is to draw out how natural death can be linked to the hero's position in the community or society that he has served. To approach this issue, which relates to the questions posed about death in battle, I return to my earlier arguments; the hero's violent death in battle shows his bravery and heroism, and it stands as a moral guide for the members of the community/society. These two functions mean that a hero's death in battle is favored over natural death. For instance, I already pointed out in Part One that the historical Doc Holliday passed away due to tuberculosis six years following the shootout at the OK Corral. However, in Ford's treatment of history, he is killed during the fight against the villainous Clantons.

In the case of *My Darling Clementine*, the alteration of historical facts is quite significant; tuberculosis, within the society and religious written texts of the 19th century, carried ideological significance. In some of these documents, dying from tuberculosis, as painful as it was, would have been regarded as a good way to die. David Ellis, in *Death and the Author* (2008, p. 120), writes on this matter, "In the nineteenth-century tuberculosis was sometimes regarded as a good disease to have, and ... it was ... often associated with the 'good' or exemplary deaths recorded in the religious journals.... It was a disease which gave its victims time to prepare for death and become reconciled to it." We learn from Ellis that one of the characteristics of natural death is that its gradual progress provides the sick individual with time to make amends for his past actions. Comparing this somewhat metaphysical approach to illness to Ford's secular 20th-century account of the OK Corral incident results in the following observation: Holliday dies heroically during the action rather than from disease; Ford thus preserves the action ethos of the genre while showing the hero's redemption from his moral shortcomings enhanced by his fatal illness. In doing so, Ford's approach to tuberculosis is similar to the second classic approach to this disease in literature. In this reading, tuberculosis/illness does not carry a redeeming feature; rather, it is a reminder of the hero's moral failures.

Natural death in the films of Ford and Kurosawa, similar to death in

Part Four—The Hero's Natural Death

battle and due to suicide, can challenge the position of the hero and other characters. Here, I will study the effects of the natural death of Tom Doniphon (John Wayne) in *The Man Who Shot Liberty Valance* in relation to the film's attitude toward the Western genre. Scholars such as Kitses and Wood have argued that this film represents Ford's interpretation of the merging of the moralities of the eastern and western regions of the United States. Ford juxtaposes the chivalry, sacrifice and, above all, conservative and traditional values of western America with the political and legal sensibilities of eastern America. In cinema, once the hero dies due to illness or old age within a specific location (be it a desert, a town or a clinic bed), his death brings generic and ideological significance to that particular location. In this regard, in *The Man Who Shot Liberty Valance*, Shinbone is where the hero's death marks the transformation of the west from a wilderness into a modern and industrial settlement. The significance of this reading is emphasized as Tom's cult of mourners[1] remembers those of his actions that have contributed to the above transformation.

The Man Who Shot Liberty Valance shows the arrival of Senator Ransom "Ranse" Stoddard (James Stewart) and his wife Hallie (Vera Miles) in the Western town of Shinbone, having come to attend the funeral of Tom Doniphon (John Wayne). Ranse, originally an easterner, has achieved his political and social fame as the man who shot dead the infamous Liberty Valance (Lee Marvin). However, Ford, through flashbacks, proves that, in reality, it was Tom, not Ranse, who killed the outlaw.

The introductory segment of the film, the arrival of the train that carries Ranse and Hallie to Tom's funeral, lasts about 15 minutes. The opening scene establishes the industrial transformation of the town as one of the core themes of *The Man Who Shot Liberty Valance*. In line with the Western genre conventions, the arrival of the train symbolizes the modernity and prosperity of contemporary Shinbone and, in effect, broader American society. Ford emphasizes this modernity as both the senator and his wife reflect on how Shinbone has changed. The town, as Hallie describes, is now occupied by "churches, schools, and shops." These cultural and commercial monuments suggest a progressive and stable American community. However, and in line with the theme of death, Ford's representation of modernity is juxtaposed with the funeral of Tom, who was a cowboy—an individual who later is introduced as the "toughest man" of the territory next to Valance himself. Regarding Tom's death, Gallagher (1986, p. 390) cites Ford's statement from an interview in the 1960s: "Wayne actually played the lead ... Jimmy Stewart had most of the scenes, but Wayne was the central char-

9. Natural Death in Ford's Narrative

acter, the motivation for the whole thing." I argue that the natural death of such an important hero is suggestive of the fading status of the conventional morality embodied by Wayne's star persona in most of his classic Western films. In effect, those who personified these moralities are disappearing alongside most of the traditional values. In *Liberty Valance*, Tom's death represents the transformation of this morality, which has no more than a historical place within the modern Shinbone and the preservation of the American ideology.

Furthermore, the character of Ranse stands in contrast to James Stewart's star persona in Western films. As depicted in Anthony Mann's Westerns and Ford's *Two Rode Together* (1961), Stewart typically played a troubled hero who by the end of the film would return to the classic chivalry and moralities of the genre; in doing so, he would help preserve the ideals and traditions that classic Western films promote. By contrast, in *Liberty Valance*, Stewart's character moves beyond the traditional boundaries of a typical Western hero. This change in Stewart's star persona is evident later in his brief but quintessential role as an aging and somewhat comical Wyatt Earp in *Cheyenne Autumn*.

Hitherto I have established that in *The Man Who Shot Liberty Valance*, Ranse is a new kind of hero with a new attitude regarding the value of the American west. Robert Pippin's (2010, p. 62) writings are relatable to my argument: "[Classic Westerns] deal with a past form of life that is self-consciously treated as gone, unrecoverable (even if still quite powerfully and somewhat mysteriously attractive) and ... the end of one sort of order and self-image and the beginning of another." Moreover, Edward Gallafent, in *Letters and Literacy in Hollywood Film* (2013), writes that "the change that Ransom brings about is the education of women and non-white Americans and with it a feeling that such a process is ordinary, unquestionable." In *The Man Who Shot Liberty Valance*, Ford links this historical death to Tom's passing, as Ranse scolds the undertaker for taking away Tom's boots. This line refers to the old cowboy's notion of dying "with his boots on," which Tom did not. The missing boots of this man, who is representative of the old ethics of the west, show the neglected and somewhat tragic position of those ethics in contemporary Shinbone, which is now in search of the truth about its origins. The newspaper editor represents a different kind of society that intends to move beyond the myth; as he points out, it is his duty to reveal the truth to the people. However, in the end the editor publishes the legendary account of the history and not an accurate version. In doing so, he perpetuates the myth.

Part Four—The Hero's Natural Death

As I noted in Part Two and Part Three, the death of a Fordian hero in battle or due to suicide functions as a moral conviction directing those who have survived the threat of death toward their generic responsibilities. Tom's natural death serves the same purpose that his violent death would have done: it drives Ranse toward his generic role in a classic Western film. The first time we see Ranse, he is already an established politician. His formal attire and his eloquent and refined manner of speech identify him as an eastern politician coming from Washington, D.C. He can use words dexterously in social and political encounters to answer the questions of a diverse range of people, from a train conductor to a newspaper reporter.

Ranse is motivated on two levels to narrate the past. First, the editor of the local newspaper insists on knowing the real intention for Ranse's visit to town. More important, Ranse also visits Tom's coffin. This visit clarifies the position of Tom's actions and death in the film. In keeping with my earlier arguments, I would say that in most films, observing the dead (beyond motivating an individual to appreciate life's possibilities) makes the observer an understanding individual who is conscious of the values he should preserve. To fathom the depth of this clarification, first I will analyze the death of Liberty Valance. I will return to the arguments of Kitses, Wright, Wood, and others who argue that the Western, as a genre, is a representation (with mythic qualities) of certain incidents of certain segments of America's past. In such contextualization of history, certain character archetypes are born. Wright (1977, p. 129) elaborates on this idea:

> The characters in a myth represent fundamental social types. The social types are located in a situation in which all the facts relevant to an understanding of their actions are known. Their efforts, of course, create new relationships, and since these links are between images of important kinds of people, the actions themselves become images of significant sorts of actions. Thus, a myth creates a conceptual model of critical social types of people located in a complete social situation and taking significant social actions, actions that form social relationships.

In this film, Ford's treatment of the primary hero's fate is different from the fate of the heroes in his earlier Westerns since society does not recognize Tom's heroic actions. *The Man Who Shot Liberty Valance* was made in the 1960s, during a period in which the Hollywood filmmaking tradition and ideological concerns were shifting. This change meant that heroes such as Tom, who were all white males and (traditionally speaking) moral, had lost their ideological significance. Wood's writings (2001, p. 41) can be linked to this point, as he argues that in Ford's last films, "achievement depended on a commitment to ideals which the society Ford lives in has signally failed

9. Natural Death in Ford's Narrative

to fulfill. But that invalidates neither the ideals nor the films." Consequently, it is not surprising that even Ford, one of the most famous directors of the studio era, challenged the codes of the genre, as the classic Western genre was, in a way, moving away from its former relevance. Tom's unheroic death due to old age represents the historical death of the Western genre in its classical sense. Beyond this point, the hero's death forces other individuals to question their past choices and actions. Therefore, Tom's death raises awareness of the effects of traditional morality on the modernization of the current society of Shinbone, though the surviving individuals, such as the newspaper editor, reject this awareness. Thus, it can be said that Ford's new treatment of the theme of death is critical of the larger part of the modern American society, not for being advanced and civilized, but rather for ignoring the older generation's contribution to the process of civic modernization. Similarly, Wood (2001, p. 41) writes on Ford's approach to the decaying popularity of the Western genre and the values that it promoted, "One shouldn't expect Ford to be able to cope with the kind of radical reorientation the failure of ideas within the American society demanded." Ford's conservative values here are the same as those in the classic Western films, whereas Wood's liberal values and ideas are of a more modern posture.

Shinbone, as the locus of action and transformation of the west, also represents the limited sphere, wherein only a few people will learn how the modernity of the west was achieved. I further argue that the ideological gap between Liberty Valance's violent death and Tom's natural death illustrates the myth needed to sustain the idea of the west. The location of the film contributes to this reading. McBride (2003, p. 626) writes on this matter, "The almost total *absence* of landscape from *Liberty Valance* is itself a statement of Ford's loss of faith in the ideal of the American frontier." Besides, in *The Man Who Shot Liberty Valance*, the Western hero and the villain are positioned at different ends of the same historical spectrum. They both live by what Valance calls "western law"—that is, being independent of the written law and engaging in violent behavior. The distinguishing line is that Valance uses violence to achieve his personal goals, which are beneficial only to him and his gang of bandits, whereas Tom will only use violence if it is for the safety of the larger community (for example, Valance whips Ranse, who is a lawyer and the eastern hero; in contrast, Tom ultimately saves Ranse from certain death by killing the bandit). I interpret Liberty Valance's death as society's need for the ethics that both Tom and Ranse represent. The community needs Tom's practicality to fight villains such as Valance. Also, if society aims to prevent the rise of villains, it should be governed by law and order. Ranse is a representative of such civic progress.

Tom's death raises an important question: Between the two main heroes of the film, whose morality is superior? On the one hand, it can be argued that since it is Tom who kills the bandit, his morality is victorious. On the other hand, he has not killed the villain in a fair circumstance. Ranse challenges the villain and his corrupt morality, but Tom is the one who shoots Valance from the street's dark corner. There is no face-to-face epic battle, presented as heroic in films such as *Stagecoach*, *Drums Along the Mohawk*, *My Darling Clementine*, *Fort Apache*, *Rio Grande*, and *Cheyenne Autumn*. I argue that Valance's death in this fashion suggests Tom's contribution to the future amalgamation of America's western and eastern ethics and codes of conduct, a point that he emphasizes later by saying to Ranse, "Hallie is your girl now. You taught her to read. Now, give her something to read about." This scene indicates that Ford is positioning Ranse and Hallie as those who will remember Tom's actions. They will be part of Tom's cult of death, despite the rejection of their altruistic attempt to share this knowledge with the newspaper editor. In a broader ideological sense, "something to read about" can also refer to educating Hallie about American history, as Ranse the politician contributes to the progress of American society and therefore rewrites its history.

In killing Liberty Valance, Tom terminates his own historical necessity as well. Kitses (2004, p. 125) writes on this point, "What Liberty's demise and Tom's fate represent is the death of the individual spirit that accompanies the institutionalizing of the territory." The irrelevance of Tom's historical position in modern society is indicated early in the film, when Ranse is told that Tom has not carried his gun, a symbol of western law, for a long time. According to this argument, we can surmise that Tom's natural death is a logical aspect of the film. He is the hero, albeit an unrecognized one. He lives outside the social and geographical borders of Shinbone in the desert. Neither Liberty Valance nor Tom will fully integrate into society: the bandit, by not being elected as the representative of Shinbone, and Tom, by losing Hallie to Ranse. Darby (2006, p. 153) reads this circumstance in the film as the "necessary sacrifice" on the part of the hero who would build the future:

> Doniphon's aborted life represents the archetypal sacrifice necessary to ensure that the advantages of civilization will be achieved. In this regard, Doniphon's unseen life after Valance's death counterpoints the line in *Stagecoach* when Doc Boone, after sending Ringo and Dallas to their idyllic home on the other side of the bor-

9. Natural Death in Ford's Narrative

der, proclaims that the happy couple has been freed from civilization's "blessings." Ironically, the unshown middle years of Hallie and Ranse and their being childless further suggest that a civilized life is not without costs even for those who do not flee from it.

Due to this sacrifice, the real hero will not be part of the upcoming lawful community. Hence, the main point is that violence is essential to building civilization; however, it is also inimical to a civilized society once established.

The next point is that, as I have already argued, an individual's heroic death in battle or due to suicide in Ford's films is always followed by hints of a romantic union or the birth/survival of a child signifying a happy, civilized future. The future of Ranse and Hallie is peaceful, but not happy. Wood (2001, pp. 25–26) writes on this matter, "The Old West, seen in retrospect from beside Tom Doniphon's coffin, is invested with an exaggerated, stylized vitality; in the film's 'present' ... all real vitality has drained away, leaving only the shallow energy of the news-hounds, and a weary, elegiac feeling of loss." Wood's comments cast considerable doubt on the value of Tom's sacrifice. As a result, it is suggestive of Ford's ambivalence toward the traditional values he aims to stand for and the idea that modern society has not lived up to the heroism of the past. On the one hand, Tom's sacrifice has aided the industrial and social progression of the community. On the other hand, it has not produced any of the traditional results of such sacrifice—for example, Ranse and Hallie have no children. In Ford's earlier Westerns, the hero, after killing the villain, would marry the woman he loved, just as Ringo marries Dallas in *Stagecoach* after killing the Plummer boys. In *The Man Who Shot Liberty Valance*, this scenario does not occur. Tom, during his final encounter with Ranse, informs him of the truth behind Valance's death. He then declares, "Hallie is your girl now."

Ford aims to depict Tom as a man who belongs to a specific historical past. Most of the values of such an individual do not transmit to the present time. In addition, Tom does not claim the once traditional reward of love and steady home; instead, he burns the house he has made for Hallie. Pye (1996, pp. 114–115) notes, "*The Man Who Shot Liberty Valance* consists of an affirmation of home, family, community, but simultaneously an implicit recognition that what sustained these 'traditional' value centers is dead." In an ideological sense, Ford's vision at this point comes near to that of Leone, as the family has lost its moral credibility. The notion of natural death is the gradual passing away of old ideas, emphasized by Tom dying peacefully rather than suddenly and violently. I link this point to the social transfor-

Part Four—The Hero's Natural Death

mation of America in the 1950s and 1960s. Ford's Western metaphorically celebrates the conservative family values of early post-war America, but these values are now in a stage of transition. Ford shows awareness[2] of these changes in his treatment of Western genre traditions in *The Man Who Shot Liberty Valance*. It is necessary for society to welcome the modern ideas of men like Ranse (a rebellious young man in the historical context of the 19th century) in order to progress in terms of law and order. Nonetheless, even as Ford accepts the necessity of social changes, he also bypasses celebrating the new society. In this film, he mourns the passing of some of the conservative principles embodied by Tom. When Tom burns down the house where he wanted to raise a family with Hallie, the location for a settled out-of-town life is destroyed, which means that the ranch, in comparison to Ford's earlier films such as *Stagecoach*, is no longer a place that is ideologically and historically feasible for raising a family.

Furthermore, in *The Man Who Shot Liberty Valance*, the idea of "home" is not found. Darby (2006, p. 152) notes regarding this lack of blissful home that "Doniphon's ranch raises the theme of finding a home, for the major characters clearly do not achieve the residential permanence traditionally thought to embody happiness." Hence, Tom's death also functions as a thematic indication that Ranse and Hallie are still profoundly affected by the events of the past. The visual sign for this argument is the cactus rose that Hallie picks from the garden of Tom's desert house and places on his coffin. There are two significant points in this scene that should be addressed. Earlier in the film, Tom gave Hallie a cactus rose as a gift; upon his death, she returns the favor. Gallagher (1986, p. 402) offers the following analysis of Hallie's gesture: "For her, the cactus rose represents Tom Doniphon and represents as well hope for the future, hope perhaps that held a dream finer than the one fulfilled. Of course, it is age looking back upon the dreams of its youth, but one might suggest too that perhaps Ranse has not lived up to her expectations." I agree with this suggestion, for when Ranse, at the film's conclusion, asks his wife if she would like to come back to live in Shinbone, she agrees by saying, "My heart is here." This "heart" can be her dependency on the town itself and on the memory of Tom's love—a kind of romantic love that, in earlier Ford films, would have been generically obliged to produce children. Darby's idea (2006, p. 172) can be related to my argument, for he notes that the ending of this film means that the "past may die physically [suggested by Tom's passing], but it remains alive emotionally to guide the feelings of those who survive." In this sense, Tom's death creates a strong emotional appeal that brings Hallie back to

9. Natural Death in Ford's Narrative

the town and the life that could have been. Likewise, the cactus rose is a signifier of the integrity and strength of Western morality presented by Tom's past actions in life. The flower has survived the harsh environment of the desert, and even the death of its gardener (Tom), indicating that the morality of the west is likewise capable of surviving the modern world and its ethics. I argue that Ford here tries to suggest that, historically speaking, society has forgotten about the true heroes of the past. Nevertheless, their actions have left their mark on the future. However, Ranse does not understand the savage beauty of a cactus rose and asks Hallie, "Have you ever seen a real rose?" This, per se, is suggestive of a bigger fact: Ranse is not capable of fully understanding how the west and its ethics and customs work. I see his ignorance as another reason why he fails to form a productive cycle of life.

As an illustration of the complex representation of the cult of death in *The Man Who Shot Liberty Valance*, Tom's death is not fully mourned. Ranse reveals the past incidents accurately; Ford portrays him as the main character who attempts to create a historical cult of death for the deceased hero. Yet Maxwell Scott (Carleton Young), the editor of the *Shinbone Times*, ultimately refuses to publish the story (meaning that the Shinbone community will not learn about Tom's heroic actions), saying, "This is the west, sir; when the legend becomes the fact, print the legend." The legend of Ranse Stoddard is politically necessary to promote the belief that western and eastern values and attitudes can fuse together in order to push the nation forward, rather than one being superior to another. Further, this saying, beyond showing the attitude of the new Shinbone, illustrates Ranse's ideological inability to create a cult of death in Tom's honor. Instead, a group of mourners is present at Tom's funeral. I have already explained that this idea means that within the narrative a group of bereaved individuals come together to grieve the death of friend/beloved, but they do not glean any approved conventional morality from the deceased's actions. Those who have attended Tom's funeral are aware of what has happened in the past. The newspaper editor, too, learns the truth, as Ranse informs him about the incidents of bygone days. However, he does not publish the story. The unpublished story is a sign that the other characters are most likely aware that Tom's sacrifice was a necessary action for the sake of future generations; nonetheless, the concealment of the story is also necessary for the same reason.

Kitses (2004, p. 125) notes that "[i]n *Liberty Valance*, Ford suggests that the mythic properties of the genre as he developed and articulated them were fabrications. His attitude towards the domestication of the West was different now. The heroic sacrifice of the pioneer is buried, forgotten, papered over by myth. There is no longer room for the untrammeled individualism that shaped the nation." Consequently, the editor's announcement about publishing "the legend" is a verbal sign suggestive of Ranse's failure to introduce the truth about the actions of the past (and Tom's role in it) to the larger society. This theme is not present in Ford's other Westerns. Additionally, the myth that is being created for Ranse suggests that even for the law to be enforced in society, the lawmen need to be violent at times. Fisher (2011, p. 182) writes on this significant point, "Power, in the Western, had always come from the barrel of a gun.... In *My Darling Clementine* (1946), the Earps can purge Tombstone of lawlessness only through bearing arms, and Ransom Stoddard is respected and influential because the collective imagination holds that he was the man who shot Liberty Valance."

The main result of the absence of the cult of death is the bleakness of the film's conclusion. Hallie and Ranse do not even attend Tom's formal burial. In *The Man Who Shot Liberty Valance*, in contrast to the majority of Ford's Westerns, there are no burying rituals. It is safe to assume that on a national level, Ranse and Hallie have contributed to the advancement of American society. Hallie, on leaving Shinbone, says, "It is a garden now," referring to the status of her hometown. Although on a personal level they cannot live up to the standards of a classic Western film, the root of their popularity is based on the fabrication of facts. Still, this fabrication should be honored in consideration of the success of Ranse's political career. In relation to Tom's natural death, this means that an individual's violent heroism no longer has a place in the Shinbone community. I see this message as a general admission on Ford's part that American history, analogous to the history of many other countries, is not free from mythification. It is also an assertion, as in *Fort Apache*, that falsification is necessary.

Ranse and Hallie have no settled home either, and, above all, they are unable to redeem themselves from their past choices and actions. Tom's death has made them shift their focus from political and industrial achievements to personal shortcomings and failures. As Gallagher (1986, p. 402) notes, "[I]t is too late. Stoddard cannot change his lie now. The consequences of his actions cannot be done, nor the falsity of his fame." The false fame is now part of Ranse's life. Campbell's (2008, p. 337) writing on ancient epics can be related to Ranse's situation at the film's conclusion: "It is not a society that is to guide and save the creative hero, but precisely the reverse.

9. Natural Death in Ford's Narrative

And so every one of us shares the supreme ordeal—carries the cross of redeemer—not in the bright moments of his tribe's great victories, but in the silences of his personal despair." This is a point that the train conductor emphasizes, while unaware of the facts, by praising Ranse, saying, "Nothing's too good for the man who shot Liberty Valance."

10

Natural Death in Kurosawa's Narrative

Nam-Lin Hur (2007), in relation to Japanese burial attitudes, writes that during the Edo period in Japan, the body of the dead person would be buried according to specific Buddhist rituals. These rituals required family members to be present at the passing of an invalid and his subsequent burial. The religious belief was that these rituals would allow the soul of the deceased to progress to Nirvana. In this sense, in contrast to Ford's treatment of natural death, illness has a significant position in Kurosawa's films. In order to comprehend the ways that natural death alters the position of the hero in *Red Beard*'s narrative, I will analyze Yasumoto's reaction to his first encounter with illness and the clinic patients.

Yasumoto, similar to Ranse in *The Man Who Shot Liberty Valance*, represents the future. Both heroes' backgrounds paint them differently from the rest of their new communities. Ranse is a law graduate traveling from the civilized east to the wild west. In parallel, Yasumoto, in Kurosawa's cinematic text, unlike the other doctors of the clinic (who are traditionally educated), is a student of Dutch (modern) medicine. Similar to Ranse, Yasumoto brings knowledge to the community from the outside world. Both heroes are proud of their education to the point of narcissism. The main difference lies in their initial responses to their new surroundings. Ranse quickly merges with the Shinbone community. He is an idealistic individual who tries to bring law and older to the community. He fits in with the society in a short time, as most of the community members welcome the changes he offers. By contrast, Yasumoto's modern education has turned him into an obnoxious individual. He prides himself on the fact that he has studied medicine in order to become the shogun's private doctor. In doing so, Yasumoto does not initially integrate with the clinic community. Therefore, it can be said that in *Red Beard* the individual who has the advanced medical knowledge initially does not share it with the rest of the

10. Natural Death in Kurosawa's Narrative

community. Keeping the modern knowledge for oneself stands in contrast to the attitude of the Fordian hero.

In *Red Beard*, Kurosawa approaches illness and natural death as social issues. Dr. Niide's teachings on poverty and social injustice initially do not affect Yasumoto. Also, since (due to government rules) the latter cannot leave the clinic, he purposefully breaks Niide's regulations in an attempt to be dismissed. The signs of Yasumoto's frustration are plenty. He refuses to put on the clinic uniform, he does not visit patients, he consumes alcohol that is forbidden by the clinic rules, and so forth. The teachings of Niide, who stands as a shaman/mentor for the hero, begin to sink in only after Yasumoto's stubbornness and childish behavior put him face-to-face with the threat of death. By this, I am referring to Yasumoto's encounter with a mentally unstable patient known as Mantis. In Part Three, I analyzed the character of Mantis in detail. She suffers from melancholy and has a murderous temper: she sexually attracts men and then kills them, similar to the conduct of the praying mantis (hence her name). She is beautiful, as well as sexually vulnerable, and opens up quickly to the young doctor, informing him that she is a victim of sexual abuse.[1] After Mantis seduces Yasumoto, she tries to kill him by attacking him with her hairpin. He is saved from the threat of death only after Niide arrives in time to interfere. This humiliating experience leaves the young doctor injured and in tears. Perhaps this is Kurosawa's way of showing that for a proud young man to become a hero privileged with mature emotions, he first needs to outgrow his ego.

Encountering the threat of death in this scene and Yasumoto's later illness teach him that he is not invincible and that, in facing the prospect of death and pain, he can emotionally and physically break down similar to other human beings. I have borrowed this explanation from Richie (1996) and Prince (1991), who argue that Kurosawa usually breaks his characters before elevating them to the status of a hero. Richie (1996, pp. 172–173) writes on this matter, "[Yasumoto] learns that medical theory (illusion) is different from a man dying (reality); that—as the picture later reveals—what he had always thought of himself (upright, honest, hard-working) must now be reconciled with what he finds himself also to be (arrogant, selfish, insincere); and, the most important, that evil itself is the most humanly common thing in this world; that *good* [emphasis original] is uncommon." After Yasumoto escapes the threat of death, he gradually begins to integrate with the clinic, visiting patients and, for a moment, contemplating putting on the clinic's uniform. Although he is still resisting the

Part Four—The Hero's Natural Death

outfit, the transformation of his position in the film has already begun, since he opens the wardrobe and glances at the uniform.

The evolution of Yasumoto's character continues in his first encounter with a dying patient in the clinic. Yasumoto is horrified by this experience, as the patient cannot breathe properly and is in great pain. This horror suggests the young doctor's lack of experience in dealing with other people's gradual passing. Kurosawa in this scene presents Rokusuke (Kamatari Fujiwara), a bankrupt merchant who is passing away in great pain and with no family members attending him. There are several significant points in this scene that merit study. First, the old man's illness is specifically identified: he is dying from liver cancer. There is a specific meaning behind mentioning this illness. One of the ways in which Yasumoto rebels against Niide is that he refuses to share his modern medical notes with the head of the clinic, who believes that this knowledge is for both the doctors and the patients whom they are treating. Kurosawa presents this maxim during the scene where Rokusuke is dying. Yasumoto, despite all his modern education, fails to diagnose the patient's illness accurately. However, Niide mentions that, after studying Yasumoto's notes, he has recognized the sickness. Therefore, having learned modern medicine does not mean that Yasumoto has absolute authority or understanding. Niide's experience in dealing with patients combined with the up-to-date medical knowledge results in the correct diagnosis of the disease. In a broader political and historical sense, this can be suggestive of upcoming changes in the Meiji dynasty toward the end of the 19th century and an indication that the traditions of the Tokugawa period should not necessarily be ignored.

The above is similar to *The Man Who Shot Liberty Valance*'s approach to American history and politics, where Ranse's knowledge of the law and democratic political establishment is useful if coupled with Tom's western attitude and life experiences. In this sense, both Ford and Kurosawa suggest that communities and societies improve when old and new traditions and philosophies mingle together. Ford expresses this ideology through the hero's death, whereas Kurosawa suggests this idea through the hero's observations of someone else's death.

Niide's main teaching in this sequence is that Yasumoto ought to look carefully at the dying patient to learn from his last living moments. The patient is quiet and does not complain about either his sickness or the romantic injustice that has been done to him. (Later, Kurosawa clarifies this second point: his wife has betrayed him with another man.) This silence and emotional serenity toward his misfortune is the lesson Niide wants

Yasumoto to learn. In this scene, Kurosawa was perhaps inspired by Dostoevsky's perspective on social issues. Kurosawa (in an interview cited in Cardullo, 2008, p. 183) said, "[Dostoevsky] has this power of compassion, but he refuses to turn his eyes away. He looks straight into suffering and suffers from the victim." Yasumoto, however, is not yet emotionally strong enough to keep looking at the misfortune of others. He is horrified and looks away once the old man begins to choke. So, the development of the young hero's character continues as he learns that even advanced medicine cannot give doctors the ability to watch an individual's death without fear. Kurosawa here emphasizes the psychological pressure that death puts on spectators such as Yasumoto.

The other significant point about this scene is that the slow and unheroic death of an ordinary person provides Niide with an opportunity to explain his philosophy about the nature of illness and death. Beyond presenting an ideology on illness to the viewers, this moment results in the strengthening of the master-pupil relationship between Niide and Yasumoto, which leads to Yasumoto's gradual acceptance of Niide's authority regarding how to behave as a socially concerned doctor. This evolving relationship between the two doctors is a characteristic of Thornton's (2008, p. 53) idea of social heroes in Japanese period films: "The social hero ... is usually based on a historical figure: lords and magistrates of the upper-samurai rank ... prominent merchants ... and even gang bosses[.] In the films, as established figures, they tend to be middle-aged or aged (a blessing for stars growing out of their lean and mean looks), impeccably dressed and groomed, benevolent, kind to children, and surrounded by younger, adoring disciples who help them solve people's personal problems." Obviously, not all the points that Thornton makes can be applied to Dr. Niide. He is not an upper-class individual, and he is not, initially, surrounded by "adoring disciples." However, Niide still counts as a social hero according to Thornton's theory on the basis that he is middle-aged, kind to children and the weak, and, above all, looked up to by others. In this portrayal, Kurosawa moves beyond an individual's background in his films. What is at stake is whether that individual contributes to the welfare of other human beings. Richie's argument (1996, p. 175) can be linked to this discussion: "[Niide's] hate of disease is one of the reasons that he is in a public clinic—the lowest of medical positions.... He does more than merely devote himself to the good; he devotes himself to a fight against the bad." Fighting the social evil means that Niide is a typical Kurosawa hero who is deeply concerned with social issues. In this regard, the socio-political implications of illness are at the center of the film. Illness and natural death can also be elevated to the status of a social problem driven by poverty and lack of knowledge. Therefore, in *Red Beard*, Kurosawa shows that although death is a reality, the social dimension of illness is rooted in poverty and the lack of education on personal health.

Niide's conversation with Yasumoto is suggestive of the ongoing fight against the tragic side of death and disease. He says to the young doctor:

> There are no real cures. The medical science doesn't know anything. We recognize symptoms, developments, we try to help. But that's about all. We can only fight poverty and ignorance and mask our ignorance. If poverty is a political problem, what has politics ever done for the poor? Has a law been passed to abolish poverty and ignorance? Behind illness, there is always a story of some great misfortune.

I read this statement as a possible suggestion from Kurosawa that social problems, represented by illness and unnecessary death, can be resolved if the political system finds a solution for them. He still maintains the humanist faith in some of his heroes.

Ford and Kurosawa both engage with the concept of illness to reflect upon the political shortcomings of their respective societies. Hence, it can be said that Ranse, in retelling the story of Tom's life and actions, suggests that the idea of the good of the American nation is (or at least might be) built on the personal tragedies of individuals. Here, Ford's attitude toward the foundation of the American civilization differs from earlier films in which communities always champion the efforts of those who contribute to society's modernization. Kurosawa's optimism is less idealistic than Ford's.

Although Niide is well aware of the limits of medical knowledge, he keeps up the fight against illness. He does so even if this fight, for the time being, does not change much for the majority of society. Prince (1991, p. 240) notes, "Death, and the suffering that precedes it, is the limit challenging Niide's work at the clinic. It is the boundary against which the doctors continually battle." This is the proof of Kurosawa's optimism, for he suggests that although the natural evil of illness and the conscious evil of bandits are different, they are always present in society. This constant presence means that moral individuals should fight them to salvage some social good. Kurosawa portrays this attitude early in *Red Beard*, as the clinic's pharmacist says to Yasumoto, "Things are difficult here. But if you wish, you can learn much for the future." Yasumoto gradually learns to be involved in this fight against illness. For the young doctor to enter such a medical and social battlefield, as I noted earlier, it is essential that he put aside his pride. By the end of the film, Yasumoto has learned how to deal with his conflicts as well as help others; he achieves the status of a hero. The latter point is similar to Campbell's (2008, p. 32) writing: "The Effect of the successful adventure of the hero is the unlocking and release again of the flow of life into the body of the world."

Yasumoto's learning experience reaches its apex when he encounters his second dying patient, Sahachi. In Part Three, I thoroughly analyzed this sequence in relation to the theme of voluntary death. Here, I consider another aspect of this scene concerning natural death. The dying Sahachi informs his friends (who are also patients at the clinic) and Yasumoto about his past life so that he can die, as he says, "with a clear conscience." The most important effect of his life history is that the suicide of his wife has motivated him to be more concerned with others' well-being. Sahachi's account of his past life changes his position in the film from another ordinary man to that of a caring individual. He has become the sort of humane character that Kurosawa champions in many of his films.

The sign of Sahachi's humanity is that, even in poor health, he keeps working in order to buy food for the other patients. In relation to the dying man's humanitarian attitude, Prince (1991, p. 241) writes, "[Sahachi] embodies the ... example of universal responsibility, of each for all. Working too hard, he has grown more ill and is now dying. The other patients are distressed beyond comfort. To them he is a saint, thinking only of others, never of his own well-being. These are, of course, the familiar terms of Kurosawa heroism, but here that heroism has become transmuted into acts of everyday kindness." Prince's conclusion is quite significant, suggesting that acts of heroism can occur in the ordinary events of day-to-day life, as seen in both *Red Beard* and *Ikiru*. According to this view, the hero does not need to be involved in world-changing actions: helping a fellow man is also a heroic act. This is another lesson that Yasumoto learns from observing a dying patient.

The lesson on heroism has three implications for *Red Beard* in relation to natural death. First, according to this attitude, the outside antagonistic force is quite abstract. The antagonist in this regard can be the selfishness of another person, or even a society, to the extent that other people's rights and well-being are ignored. Hence, this invisible moral problem replaces death through illness as the main threat to society.

Second, this new attitude toward the enemy is an area in which Kurosawa's and Ford's films differ. I have already written about the significance of the inner conflicts of the characters in the films of Ford, Kurosawa, and

Part Four—The Hero's Natural Death

Leone, where the enemy is almost always an outsider[2] who subscribes to a compromised morality. Once the villain is destroyed, the hero has nothing more to do in his struggle against the force of the antagonist. Ringo and Dallas will probably settle on a farm, as suggested by Doc Boone. Ethan returns to a nomadic life by the end of *The Searchers*. However, Ford (except in his cavalry films) does not provide any evidence that the hero will fight the villains in a future beyond the film's ending. The reason for this is that Ford's cavalry films are mainly concerned with how the west was won. Historically speaking, the struggle continued until the expansion of the frontier was complete—a timeframe that extends beyond what Ford's films encompass. This scenario stands in contrast to Kurosawa's films, in which, even if a battle is won, the struggle against the forces of the antagonist stretches beyond the story's timeframe. For example, in *Ikiru*, one playground is built; nevertheless, the bureaucracy of the government, which is the main antagonist of the film, is still at work.

The next impact of the above lesson is the cult of death. As Yasumoto learns about Sahachi's sacrifices, he gradually becomes a member of the latter's historical cult of death. It has already been argued that the formation of a cult of death can motivate a hero to fight the villain (e.g., Ford's *My Darling Clementine*, Leone's *For a Few Dollars More*) or drive the remaining characters to learn from those deeds of the deceased hero (e.g., Ford's *Fort Apache*, Kurosawa's *Kagemusha*) that are ideologically approved by the film. In *Red Beard*, the audience witnesses a nexus of these two usages of the cult of death. The young doctor, following the death of Sahachi, fully integrates with the environment of the clinic. The epiphenomenon of this integration is his engagement with battling illness. Yasumoto also learns from Sahachi's sacrifices, dedicating himself to the emotional and physical well-being of others. The proof of this idea is found in the way he treats his first patient, Otoyo (Terumi Niki), in the clinic. She is a teenager who is forced to work in the local brothel. Refusing to entertain the clients, she is beaten by the brothel mistress. This emotional and physical abuse has left her traumatized to the extent that she does not speak coherently to others. Yasumoto, following Dr. Niide's example, tolerantly spends time with his patient until her body and mind have recovered. Here, we should not ignore another element that contributes to her recovery—that is, the tranquility of the clinic environment. Prince (1991, p. 236) writes on this point, "Healing ... comes through inhabiting the special space of the clinic, a region of quiet, stability, and security so different from the outer world."

In treating Otoyo, Yasumoto becomes sick. In this scenario, Kurosawa

10. Natural Death in Kurosawa's Narrative

does not use illness as a life-threatening concept, but rather as a way to show a positive development—namely, good begets good. Once the young doctor becomes ill, Otoyo, the very patient whom he has cured, will nurse him. In such a reversal of the patient-healer relationship, Kurosawa composes a moral symmetry for his film. It can be said that the care Yasumoto has invested in his patient goes beyond her physical recovery. Her mentality toward others is affected as well. Here the threat of death is a morally clarifying force in *Red Beard*. Otoyo has, like Yasumoto, learned to care for others. The sign for this development is how well she nurses the invalid doctor, a point that is emphasized by Yasumoto's mother when she says, "You don't look like you have been sick."

Furthermore, at the end of the film, Yasumoto refuses to work for the clan as the shogun's personal doctor, therefore overcoming class issues in favor of a broad humanism that includes all those divorced from their social and class background. He remains in the hospital to help Niide with the patients. There is a visual sign at the end of the film, which suggests that, as a circle, the hero's journey and his fight against death and illness continues. The film begins with a shot of the clinic's gates, and it ends with the same shot. McDonald (1983, p. 84), regarding the presence of the clinic gate and its relation to the hero's circular journey in the film, writes, "In the earlier scene involving Yasumoto's first visit to the clinic, this gate looked gloomy and disreputable against the background of the desolate wind. But now it looks like the emblem of pride and dignity, externalizing Yasumoto's spiritual regeneration."

11

Natural Death in Leone's Narrative

In Sergio Leone's Westerns, none of the characters die due to natural causes. However, the concept of sickness holds a pivotal position in *Once Upon a Time in the West*. The death of Morton (Gabriele Ferzetti) shows Leone's attitude toward natural death. Morton is dying from what he calls "the tuberculosis of bones." His grand business concept, a railroad that will connect "the Atlantic to the Pacific," symbolizes the great historic changes that the west will undergo. However, he does not live long enough to see his vision recognized, as Cheyenne's gang kills him.

Morton's violent death is suggestive of two points. First, Leone, in following the codes of the genre, kills off his villain in a battle. Second, his death means that, at that juncture of the history of the American West (as Leone reads this history), a violent death is more likely than a natural death. Nevertheless, the prospect of a natural death suggests a threat to an individual's hopes and dreams for the future. The point, however, is to respond to such a threat by carrying out one's plan. Morton follows such thinking in striving to create a transcontinental railroad. In this sense, the concept of disease in Leone's work has a different sensibility than it does in a Kurosawa's *Red Beard*. As described in the previous chapter, in *Red Beard* sickness is nature's evil, and it can motivate the hero to undertake moral actions that benefit the Japanese society. By contrast, illness in Leone's film is not a narrative strategy to show the humane side of the characters. Therefore, Morton's illness does not motivate him, for example, to become an honest businessman—quite the opposite. Instead, the illness induces him to be ruthless and pair with criminals such as Frank to achieve his goals more swiftly. Thus, in Leone's visual text, the dying man, similar to the living individuals, is determined to achieve his personal goals at any cost. This, beyond showing the lack of humanity in Leone's characters, illustrates Leone's attitude toward the genre and his cynical moral perspective. Still, in his approach to the Western genre, it is necessary for these characters to be cold-blooded in order for society to change, even if this change does not

11. Natural Death in Leone's Narrative

mean the elimination of all villains. Here, I do not mean that Leone necessarily has a positive or a negative attitude toward the idea of a new American society. The conclusion of *Once Upon a Time in the West* does not clarify Leone's final response to the end of the west and the birth of modern America. On the one hand, Harmonica (the hero) kills Frank (the villain). On the other hand, as Harmonica argues, other businessmen like Morton will come to the west to control and shape it.

Leone's approach to building a new civilization in the west is the area in which his films differ from Ford's works. In the latter's films, for society to improve, it is necessary for moral and law-abiding people of the west and east to join forces, as in *The Man Who Shot Liberty Valance*. However, in Leone's *Once Upon a Time in the West*, a new civilization begins to emerge as violent individuals, with a sense of personal morality, treat each other with cruelty. They may be killed, like Morton, Frank, and Cheyenne, or they might move away from the newly established civilization, as Harmonica does. Nonetheless, their efforts result in the creation of a new society. The mutual cruelty of the hero and the villain does not mean they follow the same philosophy, though the difference between the characters' thinking is minimal. For example, Cheyenne, who does not mind killing lawmen, protests Frank's actions by saying, "I would never kill a child."

Leone bypasses celebrating or condemning the new town. In contrast to Ford, he does not show us the future that his characters have created. In short, Leone solely portrays the actions of these individuals, regardless of their outcome. In the final duel of the film, the antagonist (Harmonica) and the villain (Frank) have the opportunity to abandon the fight. Such a withdrawal could result in a quiet life, like Tom's later years in Ford's *The Man Who Shot Liberty Valance*. They refuse to do so, as they "cannot be a businessman like Morton," or, as Ford's Doc Boon from *Stagecoach* would say, they cannot accept the "blessings of the civilization." The hero's absence from the nascent modern society is a shared theme between *Once Upon a Time in the West*, *Stagecoach* and *The Man Who Shot Liberty Valance*. Harmonica is a substitute for the Tom and Ringo characters. Nevertheless, there are no classic villains such as Liberty Valance or the Plummer boys here; capitalist figures such as Morton have already taken over the western frontier, its heroes, and its demons. In a broader ideological sense, this situation means that Leone goes one step further than Ford: although heroes and villains face each other in a standoff, they do not have much purpose to serve once the modernization of the west begins.

Harmonica, too, only engages in acts of violence to deal with Frank

Part Four—The Hero's Natural Death

and to defend Jill. Leone emphasizes the similarity between these two characters when Harmonica suggests that he and Frank are from "an ancient race" and that they will soon be killed off by businessmen like Morton. Frank concurs with this point. In this sense, if Morton had died of illness, his death would be an ironic one since his attitude will endure through the actions of other businessmen. The old west is fading away, and the capitalist/corporate America will take its place. Thus, the historical presence of Leone's traditional characters will soon be irrelevant: the modern west will be born shortly, as indicated by the workers installing the rail tracks in the desert for the upcoming train that will bring change, regardless of its moral implications, to the west and its inhabitants.

Conclusion

In this book, I have identified and analyzed the methods through which the threat of death affects the position of the hero in the films of John Ford, Akira Kurosawa, and Sergio Leone. I have drawn on scholarly observations that the films of these men (regardless of their differences) share similar thematic traits, including those regarding the relationship between the threat of death and the hero's journey in the narrative. Since Western and samurai films are popular products, issues surrounding death, the hero's relationship to it and, above all, the ideological concerns of Ford, Kurosawa, and Leone regarding the history of America or Japan make these films a rich source of further academic focus and study.

This book breaks new ground by presenting general theories and precise observations on heroes and death in the epic drama films within a comparative cultural anthropology framework. In effect, undertaking this research and presenting its findings has contributed significantly to my academic understanding of the position of the theme of death in Western and samurai films in particular. I further realized that Leone had engaged less substantially with the symbolic and ideological issues surrounding death in comparison to Ford and Kurosawa. Nevertheless, Leone's distinctive position as a European filmmaker who made Western films spans the transnational and generic language of this book. That is why the different philosophy of his films merits further study.

To write this book, it was necessary to the integrate various dimensions of existing scholarship. The current writings on the works of Ford and Kurosawa (epitomized by the work of Kitses and Richie), as extensive as they are in their analysis of the theme of death, leave much to be desired. To overcome this issue, I integrated the current scholarship on the methods that Ford and Kurosawa used to approach the conventions of American and Japanese cinema into a broader commentary on the theme of death, both in its structural position in the narrative and in its political and sociological dimensions.

Conclusion

In order to expand the discourse of Kitses and Richie, I engaged with texts that have more to do with the theme of death in cinema and history. Among these documents, Hagin's *Death in Classical Hollywood Cinema* was seminal in forming my theory. I critically applied Hagin's ideas to my arguments, using his writing to advance my ideas, especially about the themes of the cycle of life and the cult of death.

I also focused on the writings of Musashi and Tsunetomo regarding the attitudes of the samurai class toward the threat of death in its historical and social context. One of the essential factors in their writing is that both men lived in the earlier historical eras that Kurosawa depicts in his films. Therefore, in their books, they have offered their contemporary experience of living in the bygone eras. There is, however, a dichotomy between the views of Musashi and Tsunetomo regarding issues surrounding social attitudes toward death. I applied this dichotomy to the films of Kurosawa and furthered the scholarly discussion of Kurosawa's films by explaining how I read his work in relation to the theme of death.

The books of Frayling and Kitses remain the primary sources of ideas and information about Leone's films. While I engaged with their ideas and writings, I attempted to contextualize these sources by linking them to the interpretation of the Western genre as a whole, as well as to theoretical discourses drawn from other areas of film studies. While Frayling's approach to Leone utilizes a biographical perspective, Kitses reads Leone's films more in tandem with the language of film study. I learned from both styles and tried to take a balanced approach to view Leone's films regarding the theme of death in my original analysis of his works.

I am fully aware that I have been working with carefully selected groups of films. My analyses and findings are about how death affects the hero in the films of Ford, Kurosawa, and Leone. Furthermore, I recognize that my work does not include issues surrounding the hero's death in films of other influential directors who have contributed to the formation of the grammar of classic Western, European Western and Japanese period-drama films. Directors such as Clint Eastwood, Budd Boetticher, Henry Hathaway, Howard Hawks, Anthony Mann, Sam Peckinpah, Hideo Gosha, Masaki Kobayashi, Kenji Mizoguchi, Yoji Yamada, Sadao Yamanaka, Enzo Barboni, Sergio Corbucci and Sergio Sollima have their own approaches to Western and period films. The works of each of these significant and influential directors merit their study in relation to the theme of death and its effects on the hero's moral and ideological transformations. Nonetheless, some of my arguments—for example, Ford's attitude toward the hero's separation

Conclusion

from the community—can also be applied (albeit with slight differences) to Anthony Mann's work. In addition, Kurosawa's approach to samurai codes related to winning ongoing battles in his period films is reflected in Yoji Yamada's samurai trilogy: *The Twilight Samurai* (2002), *The Hidden Blade* (2004), and *Love and Honor* (2006). Likewise, the lack of natural death in Leone's films can be observed in other European Western films, in which violent death overwhelms the plot to the point that no character can die peacefully.

There is a traditional assumption in cultural studies undertaken by notable thinkers such as Campbell and Levi-Strauss that similar archetypes exist in myths, ancient epic tales, and folklore around the world. Aspects of this view are concerned with the hero's journey and rites of passage, his encounter with the threat of death and his response to such threats. These themes and concepts also influence fiction films, in which the hero undergoes a journey that will test the limits of his physical and psychological strength. As part of this journey, he must overcome his inner conflicts in order to respond to the tests. The hero's inner conflicts can be the result of numerous factors, such as his emotional immaturity or lack of integration with the approved ideology that the film portrays.

The threat of death is perhaps the most tangible and visible of the hero's ordeals in the archetypal narrative of most genre films. So, regardless of his nationality or the historical period in which he lives, the hero experiences certain scenarios/arcs, including his battle against the villains (albeit culturally modified). The outcome of such encounters is the hero's discovery or rediscovery of his abilities.

There are two possible outcomes of the hero encountering the threat of death in Western and Japanese period films. In the first scenario, the hero is killed after defeating the villains or as he is fighting them. The hero's demise can establish the overall film's attitude toward the theme of death and its place in society. In Westerns and *jidaigeki* films, the death of the hero, though violent, is, ideologically speaking, not in vain, as he is killed either to preserve the morality of a civilized society or to contribute to the civic and industrial progress of the community.

Moreover, it is often the case that the dead hero's actions will be remembered, as a cult of death will be forged by those law-abiding individuals who, through the hero's courageous efforts, survive the threat of death. The idea of the cult of death—a universal concept—is a legacy of primitive societies that continues to influence modern attitudes toward death and burial rituals.

Conclusion

I have identified two forms of the cult of death in the classic fiction films. My categorizations consist of the historical cult of death and the mythical cult of death. The historical cult focuses mainly on a factual account of the hero's actions, while the mythical cult aims to create a perfect memory of a troubled dead hero for the benefit of the historical progress of a nation or society.

The second possible scenario is that the hero escapes the threat of death. For Fordian heroes in particular, the significance of this survival is that these heroes represent what is morally accepted within cultural and historical boundaries. As a result, their survival suggests the ideological and moral strength of those boundaries.

In most cases, the hero, following his encounter with the villain (regardless of whether he survives), is rewarded. There is a similarity between different cinematic cultures concerning the idea of reward/prize. In both Western and Japanese period films, the hero will be rewarded after he has experienced a variety of sufferings and setbacks. However, the nature of this reward differs from one culture to another, and even in films by the same filmmaker.

In the different films and genres that have been the concern of this book, the position of the supporting hero with respect to the theme of death differs from that of the leading hero. This scenario occurs because, as far as generic conventions go, the supporting hero can be physically removed from the story more conclusively, as in *Stagecoach*, *My Darling Clementine*, *Seven Samurai*, *Once Upon a Time in the West*, and other films. Nevertheless, the supporting hero is not eliminated unless there are coherent and sound generic reasons for his death. Such a hero is portrayed as an individual who has committed morally controversial deeds according to the ideology of the film (for example, Hatfield in *Stagecoach* is a professional gambler; yet his troubled past does not elevate him to the level of a villain). The supporting hero, at that crucial moment when the opposing forces of good and evil confront each other, assists the leading hero in defeating the villain(s). The supporting hero's involvement in such a venture and his likely death establish his redemption from past conduct.

The villain is usually an outside force that can enter the narrative in two forms, as either an individual or a small group of criminals/bandits who are generally of the same race or social class as the hero. The villains can also be members of a large homogenous collective whose political priorities differ from those of the community/society that concerns the hero. In Ford's Western films, this collective is usually the Indians, portrayed as

Conclusion

an obstacle that the west must overcome in order to progress civically and economically. In Kurosawa's *jidaigeki* and Leone's Western films, the collective is usually rival clans or national armies. These films support the idea of a unified nation as well. Although subject to some scrutiny in Kurosawa's and Leone's films, this scenario demonstrates how a nation seeks unity to wage war against external forces and morals.

All types of villains threaten the safety and well-being of society. They also endanger the future existence of the community, for they damage the cycle of life (a familiar concept in different cultures and works of art that refers to the heterosexual union that can result in the birth of children). The newborn babies in the films of Ford, Kurosawa, and Leone are representative of the future. However, the quality of this future varies from the cinematic texts of one filmmaker to another.

Likewise, although the villains are not privileged with their own cults of death, their deaths can inform us about the mythology of the hero, as is the case with the death of Liberty Valance. The destruction of the antagonistic force produces a conclusion with several significant facets. First, the agent/agents of social and political corruption are wiped from the film. Second, in an abstract sense, the source of antagonism is dead. Third, the society may now, in terms of civic and industrial development, move forward.

Throughout this book, I have argued that, due to the nature of Western and samurai films, it is most likely that the hero will encounter the threat of death as he faces the villains on the battlefield. His encounter with the villains (e.g., bandits) is often motivated by vengeance or a sense of ideological duty toward society/community, as epitomized in films such as Ford's *My Darling Clementine*, Kurosawa's *Seven Samurai* and Leone's *For a Few Dollars More*. However, the hero may also stand up against the outsider type of villain—for example, an army is motivated by its sense of national duty/clan fidelity, not vengeance (as in Ford's *Fort Apache* and Kurosawa's *Kagemusha*).

Also, encountering the threat of death in battle has unique impacts on issues surrounding the hero, death and the cult of death. I have observed two scenarios about this encounter in the films of Ford and Kurosawa. Leone's films, however, as I will clarify in following pages, offer an original attitude toward the hero's response and relationship to the threat of death.

In Ford's films, in cases where the hero survives the threat of death, he is the founder and representative of someone else's historical cult of death—for instance, a beloved, a close friend or a family member. Vengeance

Conclusion

initially motivates such a hero. His actions will result in the death of the villain and his associates, which ultimately contributes to the civic progress of western society. In order for the act of vengeance to be seen as justice, either the hero should be an officer of the law (as in *My Darling Clementine*) or a figure of law should help the hero in his quest (as is the case in *Stagecoach*).

I also noted that, following the defeat of the villain, the hero usually has a chance at love. Therefore, the battlefield is that ideological space where, first, justice is served through violence and, second, the future of upcoming generations is established (e.g., *Fort Apache*).

In the second case, if the Fordian hero dies on the battlefield, his death functions as a generic motivation for others to continue his quest. A hero may have gone to battle influenced by his emotional conflicts, but as long as his actions contribute to the political progress of the nation, he can function as a role model for others. In short, the battlefield is the location where those Americans who initially clash with the hero move beyond their personal feelings for him and form the dead hero's mythical cult of death. The presence of such a cult indicates that we should ignore the hero's shortcomings and view his abilities in an exaggerated manner, as is the case in *Fort Apache*. However, Ford's attitude toward the idea of truth changed over time. For example, in *The Man Who Shot Liberty Valance*, one of his later films, the location where the shooting takes place is still where the villain is destroyed. However, it is necessary to forge a myth about who has killed the villain, meaning that the true hero will lose his generic and social position in the film. Nevertheless, this myth appears to be necessary in order to make the future secure for most people.

In contrast to Ford's work, vengeance does not motivate Kurosawa's heroes (at least in his samurai films). For Kurosawa, the hero usually aims to save a friend, or someone who can be seen as his friend, from death or hardship (e.g., *Yojimbo*). Once the hero is victorious in battle and survives the threat of death, he is rewarded by gaining knowledge about his abilities as a warrior and his duty toward the greater society.

In Ford's films as well, the hero learns about his physical and ethical strength. However, the tangible rewards, such as romantic attachment and indications of a possible cycle of life, are the factors contributing to his emotional maturity. In this scenario, newborn children will be an indication of a secure future according to Hollywood's idealistic approach to love. In accordance with classical filmmaking conventions, for the American hero to be truly happy, he should be romantically (and by the customary vali-

Conclusion

dation of heterosexual monogamy) involved with a woman. This involvement also suggests an idealistically happy future for the nation.

However, since there is often no romantic love story in Kurosawa's films, the emphasis will be on the hero's emotional growth. If there is a romantic storyline, the hero's acquired knowledge about his social status puts an end to the romance. I also noted that the presence of newborn babies in Kurosawa's films suggests a potentially better future for humanity.

A further point of separation between the attitudes of Kurosawa and Ford toward the theme of death is that in the latter's films, the hero's death can be remembered through forging a mythical cult of death. As I noted, this kind of cult manipulates the facts and history to compensate for the hero's shortcomings. In contrast, in Kurosawa's films, either there is no cult of death created for the hero (*Kagemusha*) or the forged cult is a historical one (*Seven Samurai*), which aims to remember the truth about the dead hero's life and actions. This type of cult presents facts to suggest that tragedy is not compensated for with idealistic achievements.

I also argued that none of Leone's primary heroes is ever killed in the battle against the villains. The main goal of Leone's heroes, in tandem with heroes of other European Westerns, is to survive the harsh historical and financial environment in which they live. This being said, I have observed a sense of evolution in the primary hero's journey throughout Leone's career. His heroes gradually lose their interest in financial gain (*A Fistful of Dynamite*) and steadily become motivated by vengeance (*Once Upon a Time in the West*). One of the distinguishing factors of Leone's films related to the theme of death is that vengeance is often cynical and bitter because its motives are purely personal. So, Leone's individualist approach moves further from Ford's attitude toward vengeance, which in *Stagecoach* or *My Darling Clementine* has a civic value. Likewise, I suggest that Leone's primary heroes, in contrast to Ford's and Kurosawa's protagonists, will not be part of a large cult of death. While others may contribute to the hero's cause, they are usually in the dark about his primary motive of vengeance. This scenario again stands in contrast with the work of Ford and Kurosawa, in which others know about the hero's motivations.

I have further explained that even Leone's most conventional heroes differ from the classic Western film hero. I have clarified this point in my reading of the conclusion in *A Fistful of Dynamite*. The revolution is victorious, and the hero has managed to avenge the death of his sons and father and, in doing so, has contributed to the future of society. However,

Conclusion

this future is not the utopian society that Ford portrayed in many of his films. In Leone's film, the hero asks, "What about me?" His question is suggestive of his concern for his own well-being following the death of his only friend. In this scenario, it can be said that Leone goes one step further than Ford and Kurosawa, who position their heroes in situations that lead to their involvement in others' well-being. The Leone hero is more aware of his need for happiness after performing altruistic deeds in comparison to Fordian and Kurosawa heroes. In a more cynical reading, it can even be said that Leone's hero is more selfish, despite his sense of altruism.

Following the threat of death in battle, I addressed issues surrounding suicide in the films of Ford, Kurosawa, and Leone. I have discussed how these filmmakers, although motivated by different cultural and ideological conventions, favor avoiding this type of death. Therefore, in their films, in order to show/indicate an act of suicide, they position their heroes in such overwhelming situations that suicide appears to be the only tangible action to take.

I have identified two approaches to suicide in the films of these directors—namely, suicide is either an act of redemption or an act of despair. In Ford's 3 *Godfathers* and *7 Women*, the hero's suicide is acceptable under the following conditions: The hero/heroine is a fallen individual; yet he/she is not a villain. The fallen hero/heroine is somehow contributing to the future, as he/she tries to save a newborn baby from the wasteland that is a desert or a corrupt community. And the hero's/heroine's physically/sexually degrading position (e.g., being kept as a bandit's concubine in *7 Women*) is in such an unpromising state that no human power can save him/her from an agonizing death or significant emotional and physical humiliation.

In contrast to Ford's films, suicide does not have a redemptive quality in Kurosawa's films. Instead, it is a manifestation of financial, emotional and social despair that individuals encounter in their daily lives. I have argued that in Kurosawa's films, once a person commits suicide, the main fault lies with society. Therefore, Kurosawa asserts that society should show a better understanding of an individual's troubles. In Kurosawa's films, following an individual's suicide, the hero can notice the variety of shortcomings that led to the said person's suicide. In this sense, it can be said that suicide due to despair motivates the hero to be concerned with the issues that a community faces.

The next point under consideration is that Kurosawa is concerned with suicide undertaken by people of any social class, rather than *seppuku* or ritualistic Japanese suicide, which is mainly committed by the samurai.

Conclusion

I have argued that although the latter is a significant aspect of Japanese warrior and social culture, it is absent from Kurosawa's opus. I suggest that the reason for this absence is that Kurosawa, similar to Ford and Leone, transmits the message that life must be lived beyond its challenging moments—that is, Kurosawa engages with western humanism. Therefore, for Kurosawa, suicide due to honor is a tradition that should not be observed, for it is anti-humanist.

Leone, too, rarely portrays cases of suicide in his films. On the one hand, he shows an example of what I see as redemptive suicide (*A Fistful of Dynamite*); on the other hand, he shows suicide due to despair (*For a Few Dollars More*). Leone's approach to redemptive suicide differs from Ford's attitude. I have written in the introduction that Leone has his own unique and ironic representation of Western genre codes, including the codes on death and its tragic consequences. In effect, I see the redemptive quality of suicide in his films as ironic. A Leone character who commits suicide is not in need of redemption in the Fordian sense. For example, the character of Sean in *A Fistful of Dynamite* is traumatized after killing a friend who spied for the English authorities during the Irish revolution. The irony of suicide in this film is that Sean, at the hour of his death, reminiscences about his joyful memories with a friend whom he was forced to kill. By contrast, the audience generally does not witness such scenes in Ford's films, in which the hero commits suicide off-screen. In addition, the dead character's joyous ghost approaches the main hero (as is the case in *3 Godfathers*), suggesting that he is reunited with his national and ideological roots and thus is redeemed.

The similarity between Leone and Ford's approaches to suicide is that they represent the process of redemptive suicide in the same fashion. First, the hero's past is troubled. Second, he/she is engaged in an endeavor that contributes to the upcoming changes in individuals and society. Third, he/she is physically trapped in a situation in which there is no hope for him/her to face a dignified demise. Therefore, the only feasible option is suicide.

Leone's attitude toward suicide due to despair separates his vision further from Kurosawa's take on this issue. In Kurosawa's films suicide is a sign of society's failure to provide a decent life for its members. For Leone, this method of suicide is more about portraying the depth of the trauma that an individual's actions can cause rather than the failure of society to prevent tragedy in general. In *For a Few Dollars More*, a rape victim commits suicide; she fails to cope with the sudden personal and emotional changes in her situation.

Conclusion

In this book, I have also focused on the effects of natural death/death due to old age or illness in the films of Ford, Kurosawa, and Leone. Ford's approach to this concept shows the gradual demise of Western genre values in the modernized American west. The second function of natural death in Ford's films is that it illustrates the position of the traditional Western hero in society, as he dies in seclusion away from the human community. The conventional hero has no place in the civilization that he has helped build. If the hero is an outcast, the community responds to his death in a way that hides the fact that he was not part of the community in life. For example, in *Fort Apache*, the community forges a mythical cult of death to distort the facts, portraying a troubled hero as a great commander. Later, in *The Man Who Shot Liberty Valance*, the community (represented by the editor of its newspaper) blocks an attempt to create a historical cult of death for the true hero, which would serve to establish the truth. The myth of Ranse Stoddard, "the man who shot Liberty Valance," has created a historically idealistic garden at the expense of ignoring the selfless actions of heroes such as Tom Doniphon. In this context, I argue that violent death has more ideological significance in the Western genre's mythopoeia.

In Kurosawa's work, illness and natural death have their ideology; beyond being obstacles that the hero encounters on his journey, they are strategies that motivate a reluctant hero to return to his social and generic duties to other individuals. Also, the hero's struggle with illness, either his own or that of others, results in termination of his conflicts. However, I do not mean that the leading or supporting hero escapes death. The point is that after the struggle with illness, the hero is, emotionally speaking, at peace. This scenario directly contrasts with Ford's treatment of illness in *My Darling Clementine*, where the troubled hero, Doc Holliday, suffers from tuberculosis. However, this illness does not motivate him to undertake moral actions. Instead, Holliday's knowledge of his dire situation leads him to drink heavily and live a rather bleak existence before he takes up arms with the main hero to fight against the villains.

It should also be considered that illness in Kurosawa's films (and the hero's response to it) can motivate other film characters besides the hero to become concerned with social problems. Thus, illness, apart from being a cause of death, can function as the antagonistic force in the film. Responding to the presence of such evil, similar to dealing with a traditional villain, pushes individuals to discover the depths of their humanity.

Leone's films, in a further departure from Ford's and Kurosawa's approaches to natural death in Western/period films, often avoid addressing

Conclusion

this kind of death directly. In his films, people die in high numbers. Life appears to have lost its value, as the opening title card in *For a Few Dollars More* suggests. According to such an outlook, natural death and its ideological and generic implications do not serve many purposes. There is, however, one significant reference to illness in Leone's *Once Upon a Time in the West*. In his approach to illness, it does not matter what the physical pain of the afflicted individual is. The significant factor is the way that the invalid responds to his physical shortcomings and the possibility of a natural death. This point can be compared to Kurosawa's ideological approach to illness. Whereas illness in Leone's films is a negative motivation that directs the invalid to be as violent as necessary for his business plans to proceed, in Kurosawa's work, illness can convince characters to undertake socially and ideologically approved deeds.

Finally, Leone's villain in *Once Upon a Time in the West* is not motivated to atone in a moral and practical sense for his past conduct, and he continues to be a ruthless businessman. The only change is that he uses violence to push his business ventures forward. The use of direct force in this manner is another divergence between Leone's and Ford's interpretations of the Western genre. In the latter, civilization progresses thanks to the efforts of the men who intend to bring law and order to society. In the former, society progresses because individuals who seek to carry out their selfish plans engage in methods that Ford's films would have condemned. In short, Ford's characters are, in general, focused on political progress, whereas Leone's characters are mainly capitalists stripped of any concern for law and order.

I have highlighted the similarities and differences between the personal attitudes of Ford, Kurosawa, and Leone toward death and the hero's position in their films. As much as I write about the differences, I agree with Campbell's (2008, p. 33) idea that, "whether presented in the vast, almost oceanic images of the Orient, in the vigorous narratives of the Greeks, or in the majestic legends of the Bible, the adventure of the hero normally follows the pattern of the nuclear unit ... a separation from the world, a penetration to some source of power, and a life-enhancing return." These wise words stand as a testament to the similarities linking all heroes.

Chapter Notes

Introduction

1. In this book "Western," with the capital W, refers to the Western movie genre, whereas "western" will refer to the culture of American and European countries (as well as the western region of the United States).
2. Italics are in the original.
3. Nitobe published *Bushido* for the first time in 1900. On the meaning of *bushido*, Nitobe (2001, p. 4) writes, "*Bu-shi-do* means literally Military-Knight-Ways—the ways which fighting nobles should observe in their daily life as well as in their vocation; in a word, the 'Precepts of Knighthood,' the *noblesse oblige* of the warrior class."
4. Musashi wrote the original manuscript in the 17th century.

Chapter 2

1. I retrieved this article from the *Film Reference* website (http://www.filmreference.com/Films-Pi-Ra/Rashomon.html).

Chapter 4

1. The first type is "initial death," which, as I mentioned in Part One, begins the film.
2. The word *kagemusha* means the double or the shadow warrior.
3. Regarding Shingen's death, in one interview cited in Cardullo (2008, p. 81), Kurosawa said, "There are several historical versions of Shingen's death: the one I used in the film has him shot by a sniper, while others have him dying of tuberculosis or some other diseases. I thought it would be more interesting to have him die in good health."
4. In *Kagemusha*, early in the film one of the retainers says, "He [the double] is not from Takeda. He cannot die for the clan."

Chapter 6

1. Wyatt Earp, in *My Darling Clementine*, is an outsider who helps the community initially because he is seeking vengeance against those who have murdered his brother.

Chapter 8

1. This idea of the economic script can be linked to Leone's training years earlier as an assistant director working on big productions as well as neorealism films. Frayling (2008, p. 16) writes on this matter, "Leone said that he gleaned from this lengthy experience an ob-

Chapter Notes

session with the documentary surface of Italian neorealism (which made films believable), a fascination with the logistics of big-budget action sequences, a repertoire of techniques, and a determination to avoid the waste of Hollywood super productions. The efficiency of the Italian medium—budget filmmaking—strongly appealed to him."

Chapter 9

1. In *The Man Who Shot Liberty Valance*, the narrative does not forge a cult of death for the deceased.

2. The same can be said about two other films from late in Ford's career: *Donovan's Reef* (1963) and *7 Women* (1967) are both about Western-type heroes who are historically and geographically out of place.

Chapter 10

1. It is not my intention to study Mantis' case from a psychiatric point of view; nevertheless, according to Aaron Beck's writings (1990), an individual with mantis-like emotional issues likely suffers from Borderline Personality Disorder (BPD).

2. The only exception is the lack of a traditional villain in *3 Godfathers* (1948). Here, the harsh environment of the desert is the enemy.

Bibliography

Abe, Chikara (2002). *Impurity and Death: A Japanese Perspective.* Boca Raton, FL: Universal Publishers.
Altman, Rick (1999). *Film/Genre.* London: BFI Publishing.
Alvarez, A. (1971). *The Savage God: A Study of Suicide.* London: Penguin Books.
Anderson, Joseph, and Richie, Donald (1982). *The Japanese Film: Art and Industry* (expanded edition). Princeton, NJ: Princeton University Press.
Aries, Philippe (1976). *Western Attitudes toward Death: From the Middle Ages to the Present.* London: Marion Boyars.
Aries, Philippe (1981). *The Hour of Our Death.* London: Allen Lane.
Aristotle (1996). *Poetics.* London: Penguin Classics.
Bakhtin, Mikhail (1984). *Rabelais and His World.* Bloomington: Indiana University Press.
Bandy, Mary Lea, and Kevin Stoehr (2012). *Ride, Boldly Ride: The Evolution of the American Western.* Berkeley: University of California Press.
Barra, Allen (1998). *Inventing Wyatt Earp: His Life and Many Legends.* New York: Carroll Graf.
Barthes, Roland (1977). *Image-Music-Text.* London: HarperCollins.
Bazin, Andre (2009). *What Is Cinema?* Montreal: Caboose Publishers.
Beck, Aaron (1990). *Cognitive Therapy of Personality Disorders.* New York: Guilford Press.
Bordwell, David (1986). *Narration in the Fiction Film.* London: Routledge.
Bordwell, David, Staiger, Janet, and Thompson, Kristin (1985). *The Classical Hollywood Cinema.* London: Routledge.
Britton, Andrew (2009). "The Philosophy of the Pigeonhole: Wisconsin Formalism and 'The Classical Style.'" In Barry Keith Grant (ed.), *Britton on Film.* Detroit, MI: Wayne State University Press.
Buruma, Ian (1984). *A Japanese Mirror: Heroes and Villains of Japanese Culture.* London: Jonathan Cape.
Buscombe, Edward (1992). *Stagecoach.* London: British Film Institute.
Campbell, Joseph (2007). *The Mythic Dimension: Selected Essays 1959–1987.* Novato, CA: New Library World.
Campbell, Joseph (2008). *The Hero with a Thousand Faces.* Novato, CA: New Library World.
Camus, Albert (1975). *The Myth of Sisyphus.* London: Penguin.

Bibliography

Cardullo, Bert (2008). *Akira Kurosawa: Interviews*. Jackson: University Press of Mississippi.
Caughie, John (ed.) (1981). *Theories of Authorship*. London: Routledge and Kegan Paul.
Cohen, Hubert I. (2003). "Wyatt Earp at the O.K. Corral: Six Versions." *Journal of American Culture* 26(2): 204–223.
Darby, William (2006). *John Ford's Westerns*. Jefferson, NC: McFarland.
Durkheim, Emile (1952). *Suicide*. London: Lowe & Brydone Printers.
Elias, Norbert (1985). *The Loneliness of the Dying*. Oxford: Basil Blackwell.
Ellis, David (2008). *Death and the Author*. Oxford: Oxford University Press.
Erasmo, Mario (2012). *Death: Antiquity and Its Legacy*. London: I.B. Tauris.
Fawell, John (2005). *The Art of Sergio Leone's* Once Upon a Time in the West*: A Critical Appreciation*. Jefferson, NC: McFarland.
Fisher, Austin (2011). *Radical Frontiers in the Spaghetti Western*. London: Tauris Academic Studies.
Frayling, Christopher (2000). *Something to Do with Death*. London: Faber & Faber.
Frayling, Christopher (2006). *Spaghetti Westerns: Cowboys and Europeans from Karl May to Sergio Leone*. London: I.B. Tauris.
Frayling, Christopher (2008). *Once Upon a Time in Italy*. London: Thames and Hudson.
Frye, Northrop (1973). *Anatomy of Criticism*. Princeton, NJ: Princeton University Press.
Gallafent, Edward (2013). *Letters and Literacy in Hollywood Film*. New York: Palgrave Macmillan.
Gallagher, Tag (1986). *John Ford: The Man and His Films*. Berkeley: University of California Press.
Gazzaniga, Andrea (2013). "From Whore to Hero: Reassessing Jill in *Once Upon a Time in the West*." In Sue Matheson (ed.), *Love in Western Film and Television: Lonely Hearts and Happy Trails*, 53–71. London: Palgrave Macmillan.
Gerstner, David A., and Staiger, Janet (eds.) (2003). *Authorship and Film*. London: Routledge.
Goodwin, James (1994). *Akira Kurosawa and Intertextual Cinema*. Baltimore: John Hopkins University Press.
Hagin, Boaz (2010). *Death in Classical Hollywood Cinema*. Hampshire, UK: Palgrave Macmillan.
Hur, Nam-Lin (2007). *Death and Social Order in Tokugawa Japan*. Cambridge, MA: Harvard University Press.
Iga, Mamoru (1986). *The Thorn in the Chrysanthemum*. Berkeley: University of California Press.
Ikegami, Eiko (1995). *The Taming of the Samurai*. Cambridge, MA: Harvard University Press.
Jung, Carl Gustav (2003). *Aspects of the Masculine*. London: Routledge.
Kitses, Jim (2004). *Horizons West: Directing the Western from John Ford to Clint Eastwood*. London: BFI Publications.
Krook, Dorothea (1969). *Elements of Tragedy*. New Haven, CT: Yale University Press.

Bibliography

Kurosawa, Akira (1983). *Something like an Autobiography*. New York: Vintage Books.
Leech, Clifford (1969). *Tragedy*. London: Methuen.
Lefebvre, Martin (2006). *Landscape and Film*. London: Routledge.
Levi-Strauss, Claude (1978). *Myth and Meaning*. London: Routledge and Kegan Paul.
Lyotard, Jean-François (1988). *The Differend: Phrases in Dispute*. Minneapolis: University of Minnesota Press.
Mackey-Kallis, Susan (2001). *The Hero and the Perennial Journey Home in American Film*. Philadelphia: University of Pennsylvania Press.
McBride, Joseph (2003). *Searching for John Ford*. London: Faber & Faber.
McDonald, Keiko I. (1983). *Cinema East: A Critical Study of Major Japanese Films*. London: Associated University Presses.
McKee, Robert (1999). *Story: Substance, Structure, Style, and the Principles of Screenwriting*. London: Methuen.
Mellen, Joan (1975). *Voice from the Japanese Cinema*. New York: Liveright Publishing Corporation.
Mellen, Joan (1976). *The Waves at Genji's Door*. New York: Pantheon Books.
Mellen, Joan (2002). *Seven Samurai*. London: BFI Publishing.
Michelakis, Pantelis (2013). *Greek Tragedy on Screen*. Oxford: Oxford University Press.
Musashi, Miyamoto (2012). *The Five Rings: Miyamoto Musashi's Art of Strategy*. London: Watkins Publishing.
Neupert, Richard (1995). *The End: Narration and Closer in the Cinema*. Detroit, MI: Wayne State University Press.
Nichols, Bill (1976). *Movies and Methods*. Berkeley: University of California Press.
Nitobe, Inazo (2001). *Bushido: The Soul of Japan*. Tokyo: Tuttle Publishing.
Peary, Gerlad (2001). *John Ford: Interviews*. Jackson: University Press of Mississippi.
Perkins, V.F. (1990). *Film as Film: Understanding and Judging*. Cambridge: Da Capo Press.
Pippin, Robert B. (2009). "What Is a Western? Politics and Self-Knowledge in John Ford's *The Searchers*." *Critical Inquiry* 35: 223–246.
Pippin, Robert B. (2010). *Hollywood Westerns and American Myth*. New Haven, CT: Yale University Press.
Prince, Stephen (1991). *The Warrior's Camera: The Cinema of Akira Kurosawa*. Princeton, NJ: Princeton University Press.
Pye, Douglas (1996). "Genre and History: *Fort Apache* and *The Man Who Shot Liberty Valance*." In Ian Cameron and Douglas Pye (eds.), *The Movie Book of the Western*, 111–123. London: Studio Vista.
Rabinow, Paul (1987). *The Foucault Reader*. London: Penguin Books.
Rankin, Andrew (2011). *Seppuku: A History of Samurai Suicide*. Ottawa: Kodansha International.
Richie, Donald (1984). *The Films of Akira Kurosawa*. Berkeley: University of California Press.
Richie, Donald (1996). *The Films of Akira Kurosawa*. Berkeley: University of California Press.
Richie, Donald (2005). *A Hundred Years of Japanese Film*. Tokyo: Kodansha Publishing.

Bibliography

Sarris, Andrew (1996). *The American Cinema: Directors and Directions, 1929–1968.* New York: Da Capo Press.

Shakespeare, William (2008). *Hamlet.* G.R. Hibbard (ed.). Oxford: Oxford University Press.

Simons, John (2011). *Peckinpah's Tragic Westerns.* Jefferson, NC: McFarland.

Smith, Barbara Herrnstein (1968). *Poetic Closure: A Study of How Poems End.* Chicago: University of Chicago Press.

Steiner, George (1961). *The Death of Tragedy.* London: Faber & Faber.

Thornton, Sybil Anne (2008). *The Japanese Period Film.* Jefferson, NC: McFarland.

Tsunetomo, Yamamoto (2008). *The Art of the Samurai: Hagakure.* London: Watkins Publishing.

Turnbull, Stephen (2006). *The Samurai and the Sacred.* Oxford: Osprey Publishing.

Verevis, Constantine (2006). *Film Remakes.* Edinburgh: Edinburgh University Press.

Virilio, Paul (1989). *War and Cinema: The Logistics of Perception.* London: Verso.

Wakita Haruko (2006). *Women in Medieval Japan: Motherhood, Household Management and Sexuality.* Clayton, Australia: Monash University Press.

Warpole, Ken (2003). *Last Landscapes: The Architecture of the Cemetery in the West.* London: Reaktion Books.

Watkins, Carl (2013). *The Undiscovered Country: Journeys among the Dead.* London: Bodley Head.

Wexman, Virginia Wright (1992). *Creating the Couple: Love, Marriage and Hollywood Performance.* Princeton, NJ: Princeton University Press.

Wilson, Colin (1970). *The Outsider.* London: Victor Gollancz.

Wollen, Peter (1972). *Signs and Meaning in the Cinema*, 3rd edition. London: Secker and Warburg.

Wood, Robin (1976). *Personal Views.* Detroit, MI: Wayne University Press.

Wood, Robin (1980). "John Ford." In Richard Roud (ed.), *Cinema: A Critical Dictionary*, 371–386. London: Secker and Warburg.

Wood, Robin (1991). *Hitchcock Films.* New York: Columbia University Press.

Wood, Robin (1996). "Drums Along the Mohawk." In Ian Cameron and Douglas Pye (eds.), *The Movie Book of the Western*, 174–181. London: Studio Vista.

Wood, Robin (2001). "Shall We Gather at the River?" In Gaylyn Studlar and Matthew Bernstein (eds.), *John Ford Made Westerns*, 23–43. Bloomington: Indiana University Press.

Wood, Robin (2009). "Ideology, Genre, Auteur." In Leo Braudy and Marshall Cohen, *Film Theory and Criticism*, 7th edition, 592–602. Oxford: Oxford University Press.

Wood, Robin (n.d.). "*Rashomon* Film (Movie) Plot and Review." Viewed 29 August 2015, http://www.filmreference.com/Films-Pi-Ra/Rashomon.html.

Wright, Will (1977). *Sixguns and Society: A Structural Study of Western.* Berkeley: University of California Press.

Yoshimoto, Mitsushiro (2000). *Kurosawa: Film Studies and Japanese Cinema.* Durham, NC: Duke University Press.

Filmography

The Bad Sleep Well (1960). Directed by Akira Kurosawa [DVD]. Tokyo: Toho Studios.
Cheyenne Autumn (1964). Directed by John Ford [DVD]. Los Angeles: Warner Bros.
Donovan's Reef (1963). Directed by John Ford [DVD]. Los Angeles: Paramount Pictures.
Drums Along the Mohawk (1939). Directed by John Ford [DVD]. Los Angeles: 20th Century Fox.
Drunken Angel (1948). Directed by Akira Kurosawa [DVD]. Tokyo: Toho Studios.
A Fistful of Dollars (1964). Directed by Sergio Leone [DVD]. Los Angeles: United Artists.
A Fistful of Dynamite (1971). Directed by Sergio Leone [DVD]. Los Angeles: United Artists.
For a Few Dollars More (1965). Directed by Sergio Leone [DVD]. Los Angeles: United Artists.
Fort Apache (1948). Directed by John Ford [DVD]. Los Angeles: RKO Pictures.
The Good, the Bad and the Ugly (1966). Directed by Sergio Leone [DVD]. Los Angeles: United Artists.
High Noon (1952). Directed by Fred Zinnemann [DVD]. Los Angeles: United Artists.
Ikiru (1952). Directed by Akira Kurosawa [DVD]. Tokyo: Toho Studios.
Kagemusha (1980). Directed by Akira Kurosawa [DVD]. Los Angeles: Twentieth Century Fox.
The Man Who Shot Liberty Valance (1962). Directed by John Ford [DVD]. Los Angeles: Paramount Pictures.
My Darling Clementine (1946). Directed by John Ford [DVD]. Los Angeles: Twentieth Fox Film Corporation.
Once Upon a Time in America (1984). Directed by Sergio Leone [DVD]. Los Angeles: Warner Bros.
Once Upon a Time in the West (1968). Directed by Sergio Leone [DVD]. Los Angeles: Paramount Pictures.
Ran (1985). Directed by Akira Kurosawa [Videocassette]. Paris: Greenwich Film Productions.
Rashomon (1950). Directed by Akira Kurosawa [DVD]. Tokyo: Daiei Film Co.
Red Beard (1965). Directed by Akira Kurosawa [DVD]. Tokyo: Toho Studios.

Filmography

Rio Grande (1950). Directed by John Ford [DVD]. Los Angeles: Republic Pictures.
Sanjuro (1962). Directed by Akira Kurosawa [DVD]. Tokyo: Kurosawa Production Co.
The Searchers (1956). Directed by John Ford [DVD]. Los Angeles: Warner Bros.
Seven Samurai (1954). Directed by Akira Kurosawa [DVD]. Tokyo: Toho Studios.
7 Women (1967). Directed by John Ford [DVD]. Los Angeles: MGM Pictures.
Shane (1953). Directed by Georg Stevens [DVD]. Los Angeles: Paramount Pictures.
She Wore a Yellow Ribbon (1949). Directed by John Ford [DVD]. Los Angeles: RKO Pictures.
Stagecoach (1939). Directed by John Ford [DVD]. Los Angeles: United Artists.
3 Godfathers (1948). Directed by John Ford [DVD]. Los Angeles: MGM Pictures.
Throne of Blood (1957). Directed by Akira Kurosawa [DVD]. Tokyo: Toho Studios.
Two Rode Together (1961). Directed by John Ford [DVD]. Los Angeles: Colombia Pictures.
Yojimbo (1961). Directed by Akira Kurosawa [DVD]. Tokyo: Kurosawa Production Co.
Young Mr. Lincoln (1939). Directed by John Ford [DVD]. Los Angeles: Twentieth Fox Film Corporation.

Index

altruistic 94–95
Alvarez, A. 94
American army 81
anomic 94–95, 97–98, 103–104
anti-hero 14–15, 25, 28
Apache 44, 63–64, 72, 75, 82–84
archetypal hero 10, 24
Aries, Philippe 15–17, 122
Aristotle 62
auteur theory 3–7, 9

The Bad Sleep Well 12–13
bandits 60, 71, 78, 85–86, 98–102, 104, 111, 117, 127, 138, 148–149
Bazin, Andre 3–4, 30
Bordwell, David 31, 39, 102
Britton, Andrew 7–8
Buddhism 17, 19, 32–33, 43–44, 57–58, 112, 134
burial 50–51, 66, 67, 85, 122, 132, 134, 137
bushido 17–18, 20, 55, 57, 67, 85, 157

Cahiers du Cinéma 3
call of adventure 23
Campbell, Joseph 10–11, 17–18, 23–24, 28, 38, 44, 52, 63, 66, 87, 95, 105, 116, 132, 139, 147, 155
Camus, Albert 95, 118
Catholics 70, 80, 97
cavalry 16, 40, 55, 73, 82–83, 85, 140
cemetery 21, 46, 68–69, 80
Cheyenne Autumn 82, 125, 127, 163
civic progress 29, 38, 80, 127–128, 147, 149–151
Civil War 63, 70–71, 76, 79, 86, 88–89
civilization 10, 17, 42, 46–48, 50, 52, 54, 68, 81–82, 89, 117, 128–129, 138, 143, 154, 155
Clanton family 22, 40, 46, 49, 51, 53–54
coming-of-age 12–13
conclusion, of a film 3, 12, 21, 25, 30, 39, 41, 55–56, 59, 68, 74, 78–79, 85, 88, 102, 110–112, 116, 119, 130, 132
conflict: external 62, 73, 79, 81, 83, 85, 87–89, 91; internal 62, 65, 70, 72, 77, 79–80, 89, 139, 147; personal 62–63, 65–69, 71, 80

Darby, William 63, 73, 76, 99–100, 128, 130
death: dog 18, 58, 67; forbidden 16; hero 1, 10, 17, 24, 65, 67, 89, 96–97, 102–103, 107, 123–124, 127, 136, 146, 151; hour of 15, 31, 65, 67, 83, 106, 153; initial 16, 49–51, 157; intermediary 16, 64–65, 99; natural 25, 121–125, 127–130, 132–144, 147, 154–155; one's own 16; tamed 16–17; threat of 1, 12, 16–17, 19, 21, 23–24, 36–37, 40, 42, 44–45, 47, 51–52, 55, 58, 62–64, 67, 69–72, 78–80, 82–84, 86–89, 96, 99–101, 103, 105, 107, 111–113, 117, 126, 135, 141, 145–150, 152
death, cult of 17, 24–25, 43, 47–52, 54–60, 65, 67, 73–77, 83–84, 96, 98, 100, 105, 107, 108, 112–114, 119, 122, 129, 131, 132, 140, 145, 147, 148–151, 153, 157
death, theme of 1–3, 6–7, 17, 24–25, 28–29, 34, 43, 59, 61–62, 64–66, 68, 70, 72, 74, 76, 78, 80, 82, 84–88, 90, 92, 108, 115, 117, 124, 127, 145–148, 151
Donovan's Reef 158
Dostoyevsky, Fyodor 22, 109, 137
Drums Along the Mohawk 128
Drunken Angel 122
duel 88, 119, 143
Durkheim, Emile 94–98

Earp, Wyatt 13, 22, 40, 42–43, 49–51, 53–54, 74, 105, 125, 132, 157
Eastwood, Clint 4, 69, 117, 146
Edo 32, 134
epic 10, 18, 20, 35, 38, 55, 94–95, 128, 132, 145, 147

Index

A Fistful of Dollars 12, 25, 36, 45, 59
A Fistful of Dynamite 20, 25, 98, 102, 105, 106–107, 151, 153
Fonda, Henry 42, 53, 62–63, 89
For a Few Dollars More 25, 35, 59, 68, 97, 106, 110, 117, 119, 140, 149, 153–154
Fort Apache 25, 46, 49, 62, 64–65, 72–74, 76–77, 81–83, 85, 90, 101, 114, 128, 132, 140, 149–150, 154
Frayling, Christopher 1–3, 16, 35–36, 68, 70, 88, 91, 97, 106–107, 117, 146, 157
frontier 22, 40, 46, 62–63, 69, 75, 83, 101, 127, 140, 143
funeral 51, 124, 131

Gallagher, Tag 42, 124, 130, 132
gang 15, 52, 59, 80, 127, 137, 142
gendaigeki 110, 116
genre 2–6, 8, 14, 16–17, 20, 22, 24, 28–29, 31–32, 41–42, 46, 52, 63, 67, 69, 78, 80, 86, 88–89, 94–97, 102–103, 110, 117, 123–127, 130–131, 142, 146–148, 153–155
giri 18–19, 32, 66–67, 77
The Good, the Bad and the Ugly 25, 35, 58, 69–70, 79–80, 88, 97
grave 17–18, 24, 50–51, 56, 68–69, 77
group 13, 19, 35, 38, 48, 50, 59–60, 62, 64–65, 69, 71–79, 81–85, 94, 96, 98, 102, 105, 110–111, 115, 117, 131, 146, 148

hagakure 17–18
Hagin, Boaz 1, 16–17, 29, 31, 35, 48–49, 51, 60, 64, 83, 99, 146
Hamlet 42, 51–52
Hawks, Howard 4, 52, 78, 88, 146
hero: Fordian 13, 84, 108, 126, 135, 148, 150; primary 87, 96–97, 102, 104, 126, 151; supporting 30–31, 59, 62, 65, 73, 77, 83, 86, 94, 96–97, 100, 113, 148, 154; social 14–15, 137; tragic 14–15, 24, 55
hero's journey 3, 9–11, 29, 66, 70, 94, 141, 145, 147, 151
High Noon 29
Holliday, Doc 40–41, 44, 51–54, 99, 123, 154
Hollywood 1, 4, 7, 8–9, 16, 22, 31, 34–35, 38–42, 48, 51–53, 65, 88, 97, 103, 105, 109, 111, 116, 125–126, 146, 150, 158
Hur, Nam-Lin 45, 116, 134

ideology 29, 42, 51, 54, 60, 70, 72, 81, 85, 87, 90, 97, 105, 109, 125, 137, 147, 148, 154
Ikiru 15, 19, 111, 139, 140

illness 14, 23, 25, 111, 113, 122–124, 134–144, 154–155

jidaigeki 1–2, 25, 55, 110–111, 116, 147, 149

Kagemusha 25, 65–67, 78, 86–87, 140, 149, 151, 157
King Lear 15, 110
Kitses, Jim 1, 3–4, 6, 16, 35–36, 42, 46, 50, 54, 56, 59, 64, 69, 83, 88–89, 99, 103, 105–106, 117–118, 124, 126, 128, 131, 145–146

Levi-Strauss, Claude 10, 101, 147
life, cycle of 10, 12, 24, 25, 34, 37–38, 40–43, 45, 46, 47, 50, 72, 84, 91, 96, 98, 100, 106, 112, 116–117, 131, 145, 148, 150
Lincoln, Abraham 74

Mackey-Kallis, Susan 11–12, 22
The Man Who Shot Liberty Valance 25, 76–77, 90, 124–127, 129–132, 134, 136, 143, 150, 154, 158
Mann, Anthony 52, 78–79, 88, 125, 146–147
meiji 110, 136
Mellen, Joan 2, 32, 113, 116
Mifune, Toshiro 14, 32, 111
modernity 89–91, 124, 127
monomyth theory 10–11
morality, conventional 31, 40, 60, 107–108, 125, 131
Musashi, Miyamoto 17–19, 66, 110, 112, 116, 146, 157
My Darling Clementine 13, 22, 25, 40, 43–44, 49–51, 53–54, 67, 74, 85, 103, 112, 123, 128, 132, 140, 148–151, 154, 157
myth 2–3, 10–11, 22, 28, 30, 49, 52–53, 55, 65–66, 74–78, 81–82, 84, 88, 90, 95, 97, 101, 125–127, 131–132, 147–151, 154

Neupert, Richard 29, 73, 102
Nietzsche, Friedrich 20
Nitobe, Inazo 17–19, 57–58, 66
nomad 2, 42, 140
nostalgia, dynastic 29, 46

OK Corral 41–42, 52, 123
Once Upon a Time in America 106
Once Upon a Time in the West 25, 89–92, 106, 142–143, 148, 151, 155
outsider 12–14, 38, 66, 71, 75, 81, 83, 85–86, 95, 114–117, 140, 149, 157

Index

period film 2, 10, 13–17, 21, 31, 33–34, 96, 110–111, 126, 134, 137, 146–148, 154
Plato 16
plot 1, 24, 31, 34, 37, 48–49, 51–52, 64–65, 78, 82, 98, 111, 113, 147
Plummer boys 29–30, 39, 46, 129, 143
Prince, Stephen 2–3, 32–33, 66, 87, 109, 111, 115, 135, 138–140

Ran 15, 86, 94, 110
Rashomon 25, 31–33, 43–45, 49, 55–57, 77, 94, 110, 157
Red Beard 25, 98, 110–116, 122, 134–135, 138–142
redemption 13, 28–31, 33–36, 41–42, 60, 70, 94–98, 101–103, 105–106, 110, 112–113, 123, 148, 152–153
republican 53, 76
revolution 2, 6, 20, 34, 76, 94, 105–108, 151, 153
Richie, Donald 1–3, 8–9, 56, 67, 78, 110, 113, 135, 137, 145–146
Rio Grande 85, 128
ronin 15, 18, 20, 86, 111

samurai films 1–3, 21, 31, 35, 55, 66, 72, 77, 85–86, 97, 145, 149–150
Sanjuro 13, 19, 31, 45, 77, 111
The Searchers 13, 45–47, 60, 67, 95, 140
seppuku 109–110, 152
7 Women 25, 44, 77, 98, 102, 105, 117, 152, 158
Seven Samurai 32, 60, 78, 85, 95, 149
Shakespeare, William 15, 22, 52, 60, 110
shaman 11, 66, 87, 135
Shane 28
She Wore a Yellow Ribbon 85
sosei 116
Stagecoach 13, 25, 28–30, 35, 38–41, 44, 50, 60, 72, 82–83, 91, 100, 107, 128–130, 143, 148, 150, 151

star persona 125
Stewart, James 124–125
story-terminating death 16, 60
studio system 4, 6–7, 8–9, 22, 127
suicide: due to despair 104, 109, 112–115, 117, 152–153; egoistic 94; fatalistic 94; redemptive 94, 98, 112, 114, 153

Takeda Clan 65, 78, 86–87, 157
Thornton, Sybil Anne 13–15, 33, 55, 85, 137
3 Godfathers 25, 44, 98–99, 158
Throne of Blood 94, 110
Tokugawa 18, 86, 110–111, 116, 136
Tombstone 40–42, 50–51, 53–54, 132
Tsunetomo, Yamamoto 17–19, 55, 112, 146
tuberculosis 40–41, 52, 123, 142, 154, 157
Two Rode Together 125

Van Cleef, Lee 35, 117
Volonte, Gian Maria 68

Washington, George 63
Washington, D.C 63–64, 75, 126
wasteland 11–13, 22, 30, 46–47, 79, 85, 101, 152
Wayne, John 28, 63, 98, 100, 103, 124–125
Westernization 21
Westerns 1–2, 5, 16, 18, 22, 29–31, 34–36, 44, 52, 55, 59, 65, 67–68, 73, 76, 79, 81–82, 85–86, 91, 94, 97, 104, 106, 110, 118, 125–126, 129, 132, 142, 147, 151
Wood, Robin 5–6, 42, 45, 52, 56, 68, 73, 81, 103, 104, 124, 126–127, 129
World Wars 19, 67

Yojimbo 20–21, 34, 90, 150
Yoshimoto, Mitsushiro 1–2, 67, 78, 87, 116
Young Mr. Lincoln 76

www.ingramcontent.com/pod-product-compliance
Lightning Source LLC
Chambersburg PA
CBHW032104300426
44116CB00007B/885